Taryn Lagonigro

A Memoir of Love, Loss, & Unexpected Gifts

Four Clovers Publishing

A Four Clovers Publishing

Four Clovers Publishing Registered Offices: Caldwell, NJ 07006

Copyright © 2021
Library of Congress Control Number: 2021923759

Taryn Lagonigro
Ups, Downs and Silver Linings / Taryn Lagonigro

ISBN: 979-8-9853136-0-4

Published in the United States of America. Book cover design by Kristin Broek, Sofia Lagonigro, Layla Lagonigro, Genevieve Lagonigro.

Family photo in Chapter 15 by Jeff Stiefbold Photography

Headshot by Carley Storm Branding Company

This book is dedicated to Cindi, Silvana and Helen,
who each make up the woman and mother that I am.
I miss each of you so much.

Contents

Prologue

It's been more than two decades since I sat across from my paternal grandmother at her dining room table, but every detail I remember distinctly. I can recall the clear plastic table protector that redundantly covered a vinyl one. I see the little notebook she used to track her numerous medications throughout the day. I remember well, the daytime television programs running in the background - except if it was time for the "soap opera" *All My Children*, when she couldn't be interrupted. I think back to the old rotary telephone in her foyer, as well as her kitchen wall phone, and how the cord became tangled the minute she hung up. If I close my eyes, I can still smell the leftover cigar scent from my grandfather, interestingly mixed with the polished wood aroma from the out-of-tune piano. Every detail is ingrained in my brain from the little house in the center of Bloomfield, New Jersey.

But most of all, I remember that no matter what might have been going on, whatever I could have been complaining about, she had an answer. "But look Tar, the sun is shining!" "Do you hear those birds outside? They sound like they are singing." She sought out the good parts of the day, not the burdensome ones.

Luckily, she was the person sitting next to me on her porch when I found out my maternal grandmother had passed away. She hugged me tight and told me it would be ok, and I believed her. She subsequently taught me how to look for signs from my mom's mom in the clouds and made sure to tell me all about what happy things she might be encountering in Heaven. She taught me to remember the good about her, not just her final days. She always knew what to say to make things better.

Like most of the people I have lost in life, their lessons to me were realized after they had gone.

This paternal grandmother; who we lovingly called "Ba", was teaching me to look for the small, beautiful things in life among the chaos. Eventually she was slowly losing her life to emphysema, yet the sun was still shining, the birds were still singing and she enjoyed the times with those around her. I don't remember one moment where she didn't have a genuine smile on her face.

I would lose "Ba" when I was a senior in high school. Too early for me, for sure, as I had so much more to share with her. A certain, albeit normal, twinge of jealousy would affect me when my friends would have their grandmother at their college graduations and weddings. Those beautiful "four generations" pictures that they took when they welcomed their own children and still had their grandmother in their life, were equally difficult.

Because we lived near each other, we spent so much time together. I was comforted in my knowledge that my grandmother had given me so much in those 18 years that it would be unfair to feel like I got jilted. I would do as she did, and thus remember all the good things about her, not what I lost.

It would be years before I would fully unlock the magnitude of that gift she gave me, hidden away until I found what I call a "gratitude practice" of my own. My grandmother had been looking for the silver linings her whole life, no matter what was going on. She may not have had a "gratitude practice" in the way we define it now, (as one will see at the end of each chapter here), she just lived it in her bones.

Our life seems to be woven threads of experience. We cannot protect ourselves from every heartache or every difficult moment. Unfortunately those things will always be there; bumps in the road, as it were. Stress, worry, loss. Pain, grief, shock. But while these may be a part of life that we cannot avoid, we can hone in on the beauty within each unique experience to carry us through. The silver linings are always there, we just have to look for them.

A gratitude practice started for me as simply jotting down a few things I was grateful for each day. In the beginning, I would write the same general things. "I am grateful for my family." "I am grateful for my house." These were, of course, the things I was grateful for at the end of the day. But as I developed this practice, I tried to be more specific, and that's where things started to change for me. Maybe the day on the outside was a hard one, but when you "squint" your eyes, look really close, there was good to be found. Maybe I would lay my head down on my pillow feeling like I didn't get it right, but would remember the laughter at the dinner table or the smile I got at school pickup. Those were the things that mattered.

This was not about only seeing the good. I would find that by acknowledging what was demanding about the day or letting myself feel the stressful things that were going on helped me to leave them behind and focus on the good.

Now, gratitude for my life is something I try to hold in my heart every day. Not just in the happy times. Not just the Thanksgivings or the New Year's Eves when reflecting back on them as a whole. Gratitude for me is like the air I breathe or the blood running through my veins. I try to feel it always and look for it when things feel somewhat insurmountable.

I have written this book as a collection of experiences to hopefully inspire you to find the small, beautiful things in life. While part of this book deals with some heavy losses and stressful times, I hope that when you read it you too can see the silver linings. Each story is coupled with a gratitude journal of very specific things I am grateful for with that particular experience. I hope you will see my gratitude even during incredibly trying times and know that after those storms, the sun came out again.

Most importantly, I hope when you see the clouds, you can always find the silver linings.

Chapter 1

Learning to Live
Bravely and Beautifully

There's a quote by the American writer and poet Frederick Buechner (1926-) that reads, "one life on this earth is all we get, whether it is enough or not enough, and the obvious conclusion would seem to be at the very least we are fools if we do not live it as fully and bravely and beautifully as we can." His words are among my mantras for life and have served as a reminder through times when settling or taking the easy road would make more sense.

I was fortunate to grow up with a father who, to this day, lives young at heart. My dad never lost his curiosity for life, love of learning, and zest for fun. He used to say that he would never be rich, because he loved spending time with his family too much. He was responsible, of course, and provided for us well via the small business he owned with his father, but was an incredibly present parent while doing so. In the 1980s, when the more hands-on version of fatherhood was just emerging as more "normal," my dad was serving as the PTA president, attending every school conference, coaching basketball and softball and fostering our love of learning. He would make trips to Barnes and Noble feel exciting and never skipped a ride down the water slide. He had a vision for his life and it was to live it for memories and not only money. He worked to live, not lived to work. Some may argue that way of living can be reckless, but as his daughter, I'm grateful that's the way he chose to live it.

I have always been ahead of my time being keenly aware that life is short, but not in a depressing or morbid way. I use this understanding to be present during good moments and to motivate myself to keep pushing to the potential I have wanted for my life. It was never about being "the best" at anything but more so being the best version of me. I also try to look for the good parts of hard times, to try to maintain a balance during life's stressful moments.

My favorite part of this "knowledge" I've attained is knowing that you're in a good moment when you're in it. Sometimes you build moments up and they disappoint you, but sometimes it's those small moments that catch you off guard that are the most beautiful. I try to remember to stay present so I don't miss them—a practiced perception.

The first time I remember feeling this was when I got to witness some "firsts" with some of my favorite people. With my mom, this was when I was ten and she and I attended a Paul McCartney concert at a large football stadium in New Jersey. With my dad, it was eleven years later for Bruce Springsteen at the same location. Both had been lifelong fans of each of those artists, but life had never allowed them a chance to see them perform live. I also got to be there when my husband went to Disney World for the first time; an opportunity he didn't have as a kid. In each of those moments, I remember looking over at them and seeing huge smiles on their faces. I will never forget those looks. In those moments I didn't see a tired, worried parent, thinking about bills and house repairs and helping with homework. I saw someone watching a dream come true. I have made it an intention to always take a mental picture in happy moments. There to stop and "soak it in" rather than letting it pass by. It's my favorite part of motherhood too, to watch the joy in the simple moments.

When you look for the beauty in life, you find it more and more. Someone helping another person. Your favorite meal. A smile. The warmth of the sun. It's always there, whether you notice it or not, and it's much more fun to take a moment to look for it. In time, these things become more visible.

For so long, I felt like I lost this. I did everything one was supposed to do. Attended college, got a job, fell in love with my best friend, got married, bought a house, and had two kids. I had such a beautiful family with my husband Raffaele. Everything on paper was good. If I just looked at the big things, all was perfect, but the little moments of joy were somehow missing.

I don't think there was one particular moment that I realized I wasn't happy, but more so a culmination of many months (or years) of neglecting myself. My first year or two of motherhood with my oldest daughter Sofia was easy. We had an endless amount of help from my mom and mother-in-law. They would take turns watching Sofia during the day while I went to work. I would come home to a clean kitchen, folded laundry and most importantly, a happy kid. I didn't feel much guilt working because she was with one of her grandmothers, who loved her more than anything. Someone was always around for date nights and whatever else we needed. We had a very spoiled entry into the parenting world.

A lot of that changed when we welcomed Layla. She was the easiest, happiest baby in the world but born during a time where so much in our life changed. Both of our mothers started to have some issues with their health, we were doing a major home renovation, and Raff opened his own business all around the same time. Things were stressful, and my life with two kids felt like I was on a hamster wheel with no way to get off. Wake up with the kids, morning chaos, daycare drop off, work, daycare pickup, dinner, cleanup, bedtime, repeat. I would leave daycare in the morning feeling like I had just run a marathon. My heart raced once I was back in the car, and the day had barely gotten going. My job during that time was not stimulating and I had no hobbies or activities outside the house other than work and things for the kids. How could I? I had no time.

Feeling like everything had to be perfect, this meant that I never stopped moving. I was throwing extravagant parties for my kids that I would stay up for weeks preparing for, because that's what I felt like I had to do. I would try to pretend that I had it all together, especially in the super competitive mom world I found myself in. Even with a husband who shared the duties it was just impossible to live life that way. I kept feeling like motherhood was something that I had to pour myself into completely to be successful. This couldn't be what it was all about, could it? Was I living to work rather than working to live? Was I enjoying anything about life?

Not surprisingly, I fell into a deep period of depression and anxiety. Few people in my life knew at the time, because it was hard for me to articulate. I had everything I ever wanted, what could I possibly be depressed about? Anxiety makes me turn inward, so I manifested worries about myself and the kids that were completely unrealistic, but would nonetheless keep me up at night. I became triggered by anything that involved illness or death. I started to become fearful of any doctor's appointments and any strange feeling. I was worried something would happen to me, that life would pass by, and I would have not enjoyed a single moment of it.

I was not the mother I wanted to be. I was the mother I felt like I *had* to be, and I felt myself withdrawing because of it. As the daughter of someone who battled depression her whole life, I was falling into the same pattern she did, and I knew from experience that it would cost me and my kids many happy experiences. My mom had missed many things over the years because of her depression, and I was fearful that would happen to me. Yet, I couldn't find a way to pull myself out of it. This mountain felt too high to climb. Where would I even find the time to get better? How would I even find the courage to start?

One weekend in the summer of 2015, we took the kids to an amusement park in Pennsylvania called Sesame Place. As longtime fans of Sesame Street, the tv show, this was a place we loved to come as a family several times a year. I looked forward to it as much as they did, because I loved seeing their faces as they took it all in. But this time, as Sofia and Layla enjoyed the time of their lives, I cried the entire time behind my sunglasses. I was so incredibly low that I couldn't even savor my children's joy. I felt like I was jumping out of my own skin that day, for no other reason than the confusion that was going on inside me. The girls likely had no idea, but I know I wasn't present the way I wanted to be. I felt like I was out of my own body, watching the inherent joys of motherhood crumble.

What was this? What was I doing? This "cost" - missing out on life - was too important not to take the first step to climb the mountain to feel better. As we drove home that day, I committed to myself and Raff that I would start fixing it.

That following week, I did what I knew how to do well; which was make a plan. I never felt like I had the time, but "finding" the time was suddenly of tantamount importance. I set up an appointment with a therapist and signed up for a nearby fitness studio. Exercise had always made me feel good mentally, so I knew this had to be a component of it. I felt excited for the first time in a while. That day at Sesame Place with my kids was my mental "rock bottom" and I was ready to head upwards.

The journey was not a quick one, however—they never are! Therapy is an important piece of the puzzle but it is never a quick fix. You just want to hit the fast forward button and feel better, but it doesn't work like that. It took months of therapy, exercise, yoga and, yes, for a little while, medication. I fought the idea of medication for so long because it felt like giving up. But realizing that it was only a bridge while I worked on everything else helped me to accept it. It was one part of what helped me get to a place where I could begin to find myself again.

One night, I decided to take a yoga class at the fitness studio I joined. I had taken yoga classes previously, in other gyms and even at a little studio in Sydney, Australia, years ago while studying abroad. It always felt good to me but I had no further expectations when I walked in and attended the class on that Wednesday evening. I was in the thick of my recovery and "mom guilt" was still in full force. Going to yoga that night meant missing the girls' bedtime. For even one night, after working all day, that was hard for me to do. But I rolled out my yoga mat and started to move.

What I found that night was monumental in my recovery, like the flip of the proverbial switch. My over-active mind shut off for the first time in years. I wasn't thinking about the lunches that needed to be made, the dishes in the sink or the schedule the next day. I wasn't thinking about what I didn't do right or what worry was keeping me awake at night. I was feeling strong and centered rather than weak and disconnected. I had only to move and breathe. I truly felt relaxed for the first time in motherhood. I was pleased to find that feeling also carried beyond that one yoga class.

What I started to realize was that by taking small amounts of time away, I was better overall for my family. I had spent years thinking that the only way to be a good mom was to be with my girls every single moment I wasn't working. While I might have been physically there with them, I wasn't truly present because of all the stress I was carrying. But just like I have to work and make money to help support my family, caring for myself is an equal component of this support. This is when I started prioritizing self-care just the way I would any other human need, and it has truly made all the difference.

Yoga specifically is what I found made the most impact on my mental health. It gave me a deep awareness of my body and my mind. It changed my life. Since finding yoga, I have never fallen into such a deep depression as I did that year. I now know how to "right-course" when things are going awry. I may not get to do yoga as often as I would like to, but it's the first place I head when I feel my mind start to shift in the wrong direction. The stress will always be there. The worry, the sadness, the guilt; these things will always be a part of life. I just know how to manage it better now.

That time in my life, pulling myself out of depression, was as important as anything I've ever learned. I wouldn't change the course of it all because it brought me to where I am. By truly realizing how low I was, I knew where I wanted to be. I threw out the stale version of the "adult" paradigm that I had adopted for myself and started living life in a more purposeful, intentional way. I refused to accept that age or number of children would have an impact on pursuing dreams, so I allowed myself to dream big in so many areas of life. I also started to really focus on making the most of my life and being grateful for the small "wins" as much as the big ones, the blessing that they may be.

Silver Linings:

- I am grateful that I went through this depression, because I am able to recognize the signs when I feel stressed and overwhelmed, and get control of it much sooner.
- I am grateful that I learned these lessons before some of the most stressful years of my life, because these lessons were the tools to manage them.
- I am grateful that my children were very young when this happened, with little memory of an unhappy mom.
- I am grateful that I learned so much about the mother I wanted to be, and not the one I was trying to be.
- I am grateful that my mom never hid her struggles, because I was able to identify what I might lose out on.
- I am grateful that my father showed me early on what things were truly important in life, to help guide in the way I choose to live my life.

Chapter 2

A Parisian Reminder

In November of 2015, I was asked to go to Paris, France on a business trip. I had an incredible amount of anxiety about this trip, because it was the first long business trip since becoming a mom, and I was leaving the country no less. I had worked myself up so much about it that I even asked my doctor to prescribe me some anti-anxiety medicine for the plane ride, just in case I needed it.

Once I arrived in Paris, I decided to embrace it. I had never been in this beautiful city before and immediately got caught up in its history. I spent my one non-working day exploring seemingly every inch of it and clocked about 20,000+ steps on my Fitbit exercise calculator. French architecture, French culture and French wine, it was all perfection.

After several days of company meetings, we had one final night before the early morning flight. I hadn't seen the Mona Lisa yet or the Eiffel Tower at night and felt like I would be doing a disservice to my otherwise immersion into French culture by heading home without checking those boxes. I convinced my co-worker to pay the expensive entry fee to the Louvre and navigated through until we saw the tiny painting that history has made so large.

We headed to the famous Avenue des Champs-Élysées to eat and then took the ride-share service Uber over to the tower. It was just as magnificent as I thought it would be in the clear Paris evening, but it was also very cold out, so the visit was short lived.

As we waited for another Uber, we started hearing a lot of police sirens. Having worked in New York City for many years, it wasn't strange to hear this, but I think I noticed it more because of the distinct sound of Paris police sirens.

In the Uber, I started to get texts from the United States asking if I was ok. "I saw the news, are you safe?" Confusion was my first feeling. My coworker started to get the same texts. It was hard to get a good signal on my phone but eventually I pulled up a news article that there were active shootings popping up in multiple locations—right here in Paris!—right now! Panic started to set in and that anxiety I had released since arriving came rushing back.

The Uber driver was urgently trying to get us to our hotel. Paris is full of underground tunnels and I felt like they seemed never ending that night. My memories of that drive make it feel about an hour long but I honestly think it was five to ten minutes. When we made it back to the hotel, I rushed back to my room, locked every lock and started trying to reach my family, who had obviously been trying to reach me. At this point, the entire incident was still unfolding and I learned that some of it was going on mere blocks from my hotel. I felt like I couldn't relax, because there was no understanding of whether the situation was still unfolding or under control.

I was due to fly out the next morning but the information coming out was that all borders were closed. The airline did not have information, nor did the US Embassy. I honestly thought I was going to be stuck in Paris when I had been so desperate to fly home to my girls.

Morning came and while the terrorists were still at large, the airport was open albeit with heavy security, so I was able to get out on my planned flight. Even my arrival at Newark (NJ) airport, was shrouded in security. I can't describe the feeling of coming in the door and hugging my girls.

The entire experience was such a strange feeling to reconcile. What if I had changed course that night and went to eat near the hotel instead? The reality is I was never in harm's way, but the feeling of being stuck in a strange city while a terrorist attack was unfolding gave me nightmares for a long time. I couldn't stop thinking about the people—innocent victims, who were there that night. It reminded me how precious life is.

The Monday after that trip I signed up for a 200-hour training program at my local yoga studio. This had been something I had been thinking about for so long, but finally found a reason not to put it off any longer. It wound up being the experience of a lifetime, one that led to many other experiences and opportunities, including becoming the co-owner of my own studio, Iris Yoga in New Jersey.

When I was in the pit of depression, it was yoga that pulled me out of it. I wanted to share that with others. I wanted to help other moms who found themselves where I was-- To live in a more intentional way.

While I am by no means grateful that there was a terrorist attack in Paris that night in November, I am grateful for the reminder that life is short and to take chances and opportunities.

I will always carry with me in my heart the people who were lost that night and will try to make change and spread kindness as a result of that fateful time. Maybe there isn't good in every situation, but you can take a horrible situation and find ways to create good from its memory

Silver Linings:

- I am grateful that I conquered my fear of traveling without my kids, even though it was a hard-learned experience.
- I am grateful to have had a chance to see such a beautiful city, both in its innocence and after the attack.
- I am grateful that I was able to turn a tragedy into doing well and spreading kindness through yoga.
- I am grateful for the reminder that life is short and to take chances and opportunities when you can.
- I am grateful for the sweetest hugs I have ever known when I walked in our front door after that trip.

Chapter 3

Mom's Unrealized Lessons

My mother was the daughter of an Ivy-league edu-
cated mother and an alcoholic, abusive father.
When she was seven, my grandmother took my mother
and her six siblings and left their father from their
marital home in Georgia as she made a new life in
her original home state of New Jersey. To rebuild her
life, she had to temporarily place some of her children
in an orphanage. I always think of the courage and
heartache that entire experience must have held for my
grandmother. My mother spent many months in this
orphanage while she waited for her mother to come
back and get her, and two other siblings. As a mother
now, I struggle to imagine the trauma that this single
experience would have created for a child, let alone

the other developmental disorientation that went on before and after that. I think about my mom as a little girl, dealing with such emotional weight, and it always brings tears to my eyes.

Nothing about my mom's life was easy. Although my mom and her siblings were eventually reunited under one roof, their family struggled with my grandmother as a single mother with seven children. One could have looked through a single lens and passed judgment on her for being unhealthy and sometimes (or maybe more than sometimes) brash. But underneath all of that was someone who never learned to love herself, because she was never shown that as a child, and was ravaged by a clinical depression nearly impossible to pull out of for most of her life.

As a child and then a young adult, it was hard to reconcile why my mom couldn't just be happy. She would miss out on things because of her depression and fell into an unhealthy lifestyle. While not a psychologist, I believed, and it was commonly believed, almost all of her issues were rooted in her upbringing, so why couldn't she leave that behind? She had a loving husband, two healthy daughters and a comfortable life - a far cry from the life she had as a child. She had us! What else mattered? Her life on paper was everything she dreamed of. There were times we would talk about that, and she would explain that it was not that simple. It was only after battling my own depression that I realized how impossible it is to just "snap out of it." I found myself with the same things on paper, sans her traumatic upbringing, and depression was still hard to rise above.

It was only after her death that I realized that my mom spent her life ensuring that my sister and I could have better than she had. In some simple ways, that meant making sure we always had new clothes and never went hungry. The meals she cooked were a far cry from the ones she had as a child, and my sister and I never wanted for anything. In more profound ways, it was finding a father for her children who could not be more different than the father she was given. In still other ways, she wore her faults on her sleeve for us to see and want different for ourselves. Where some people fall into and repeat their circumstance, my mom made sure that we never felt a moment of the past she endured. The selflessness of motherhood defined.

However, it was in my thirty-seventh year that the most important lesson she gave me was one I never realized I would need. My mom had a twin brother named Robert who was born with a developmental disability, an unclassified genetic condition, was the conjectural diagnosis at the time. Growing up with a brother with a disability in the 1950s and 60s was anything but easy, she would tell me. The world then was a harsh place for someone like him; not to mention his siblings. My mom, as his twin and biological protector, found herself standing up for him even as a young child. She was an early advocate against the "R" word. Back then, there was little support or therapies for this disability, and advocates weren't celebrated the way we'd like to think they are now. Having a family member with a disability could bring shame and embarrassment—both real and imagined. But still, my mom never left her brother's side.

When her mom, my grandmother, passed away in 1992, my mom became, by court decree, Robert's full time legal guardian. Maybe it sounds obvious that she would step into that role, but at the time my mom was raising a ten- and six-year-old and both her and my dad were working full time. It's incredible for me to think about the exigencies of her wholeheartedly taking on that role. Robert came to live with us for a while until my mom found him a place to live, with supervision, as was her mom's wishes. This had to be close enough that he could see us regularly. I would be lying if I said it wasn't hard sometimes to have him living with us when I was at the confusing age of ten, but I know that these were the first moments that showed me an unconditional love for someone different than myself. Yes, Robert had been there our whole lives, but watching my mom make space for him in her already busy life demonstrated how to always "show up" for someone in need.

Looking back, I know that having Robert in my life shaped who I am, in both a real and subliminal way. I didn't just learn not to say the "R" word--but knew why; and learned how to find my voice speaking up against it. I learned how to have patience for someone who needed more time. This is how it always was; having someone in my family with a disability was quite normal. Robert was my uncle, he was a human being, worthy of love and respect the same way anyone else was. He had feelings and emotions and empathy. He was who he was meant to be and his life was important. All of that should be obvious, but even today it isn't always understood. It's a lesson that can't always be taught as significantly as living among and loving someone with a disability.

As years passed, I witnessed my mom grow as an advocate, always ensuring Robert got the right care. Endless phone calls, doctors' appointments and yes, worry. My mom, much like her mother, never walked away from Robert. Although her mom had passed away somewhat suddenly, she knew my mom would look after him and I believe she would have been proud of the choices my mom made. Even when he moved out of our house into assisted living, mom fought for him to be nearby so he could spend every weekend with us. The state-supported program would have located him hours away and my mom couldn't bear that thought.

When I found out, years later, that my daughter Rhea would have Down syndrome, it was hard for my mom to see beyond all of the struggles that her brother suffered, even though it was an entirely different diagnosis. She grew up with him at a time when there was no early intervention or proper understanding of people with disabilities. There was bullying and discrimination in many different ways. Her brother, quite frankly, had no chance of living up to his potential; and that was not for lack of love from his family. So while my mom was in the early days of advocacy, equality and proper care, it was hard for her to understand that I was entering this disability world at a vastly different time. It was hard for her to not want to protect me from dreaming too big for my daughter and worry about the adversity our family might face.

The minute Rhea was born; I know a lot of that changed for my mom. I could see the joy that my mom felt from interacting with Rhea, even if that was sometimes only over Facetime. If I didn't text her a picture one day, she would message me that night, "I didn't get any sunshine today." I know she was continually amazed at the wonderful things Rhea was doing at such a young age. But beyond that, I know my mom realized that my love for Rhea would not be dependent on what she did or didn't do. She loved seeing me grow into my own advocate role, as she told me many times. I wish I had a chance to tell her how much her advocacy was ingrained in me without me realizing it. Being the sister she was to her brother prepared me to be the mother I am. It was one of the greatest gifts of my life.

Silver Linings:

- I am grateful that my mom turned her life's struggles into being a good mom, wife and sister.
- I am grateful that my Uncle Robert taught me how to love someone with a disability and have a greater patience, understanding and openness to differences.
- I am grateful that my mom was such an important example of advocacy and unconditional love. Her lessons will carry me through a life of advocacy for my daughter.
- I am grateful that my mom had a chance to know Rhea and be changed by her. I hope she left this earth feeling more confident in Rhea's future.

Taryn Lagonigro

- I am grateful that my mom rose above her circumstances and gave us the best life, despite how she may have been feeling many days.
- I am grateful that my grandmother had the strength to leave her husband, because my mom's life would have been even harder otherwise.
- I am grateful that my mom lived as an example, in both positive and negative ways, to teach her daughters so much by sometimes saying so little.

Chapter 4

2016 - The Highest Ups and Lowest Downs

In the long list of my mom's difficulties; her health was the biggest struggle in the latter part of her life. Beginning with bouts of bronchitis and pneumonia that would land her in the hospital for a week at a time, it soon discovered that she had serious heart issues. In 2016 things really took a turn when she needed open heart surgery to replace a valve in her heart. This was frankly the first time our immediate family had a major surgery like that to handle. It was hard to watch my mom feel nervous leading up to it, especially the morning of the procedure, in pre-op. It's hard to watch your parents be vulnerable, and here she needed us to bolster her courage as she had for us so many times. She bravely went into surgery and we held our collective breath for that very long day. I will never forget the feeling of the surgeon coming out of the recovery room to tell us everything had gone well. It was a feeling of relief that I had not felt before in my life. I went into the bathroom and called Raff, crying my words and releasing the fear I didn't know I had built up in my mind. It was painful to see her those first few days after surgery – breathing with assistance, "intubated", with so many wires attached to monitor her vital statistics-yet it was a possible foreshadow of things I would go through many years later.

Mom's recovery from open heart surgery continued from there as fairly straightforward, but about a month after surgery she had to return to the hospital for a possible infection. She called me one morning, a day before being cleared for discharge and mentioned she had fallen overnight on her way to the bathroom in her room. I didn't give a ton of thought about this incident at the time, other than to remind her to be careful. My mom was a klutz, so this wasn't totally shocking. But still, I brought my laptop and went to work from her hospital room that day to keep her company.

For a few hours, we sat there, and I wasn't quite sure why I had rushed up there. She was having some pain from the fall but was otherwise okay. We watched some bad TV and made jokes about the awful hospital food to pass the time.

What happened next still feels like a blur all these years later. A few doctors came in and said something about internal bleeding and that they were moving her to the ICU for monitoring. Huh? I remember feeling very confused since my mom was acting totally normal. As they prepared her to be moved, I will never forget the fear in her eyes as she looked over at me, equally confused and scared. The floor doctor pulled me out of the room and suggested I call my dad to immediately come to the hospital. That's when the shivering anxiety started to build up in my body; because I knew suggesting her husband come to the hospital is one of those things doctors say when they don't want to say how serious things are. I pressed the doctor and she explained that because my mom was on blood thinners having so recently had open heart surgery, they were concerned they wouldn't be able to stop the subsequent internal bleeding from her fall.

I called my dad and my sister Lauren and suggested they come over as calmly, yet promptly as possible. That was the first day I took on the role as "The Strong One" in this new support team we unexpectedly found ourselves in. Was it a defense mechanism? Probably. But taking charge of this situation as the one who held the team together is precisely what held me together.

After they both arrived at the hospital, and we were at my mom's bedside in the ICU, we were all still confused, or maybe in a bit of denial, as to what exactly was going on. She was still acting normal, albeit fearful of the nature of the concern. The serious Intensive Care Unit (ICU) team told us they were going to put her on a breathing tube and sedate her to allow her body to rest so they could attempt to control the bleeding. They asked us to leave the room while they got her set up on several machines and IVs. We told her she would be "OK" and repaired to the waiting room nearby and did just that...wait. We passed the time the only way our family knows how - by making jokes and eating food. I think we had just about every treat that the in-hospital Starbucks offered and were sustaining ourselves on that and coffee. We were concerned with what was going on, but I don't think any one of us thought it was life-threatening.

A while later a doctor came to find us and sat down in the room to talk to us. She said a whole lot of things, but she suddenly said a sentence that jolted us back into reality. "Cynthia needs a lot of luck." That's the moment I realized that I might lose my mom that night. April 7, 2016.

She needs a lot of luck. She needs a lot of luck! I'll never forget the sound of those words. Suddenly the jokes stopped; and faces paled.

I walked away from the waiting room to call Raff. At this moment I needed not to be The Strong One right now, and he was the only one I could do that with at the moment. I filled him in and then my voice cracked.

"I think I'm going to lose my mom. What am I supposed to tell the girls?" He didn't answer because he couldn't. The thought overwhelmed us.

Our families were not ones who only saw each other on holidays or the occasional Sunday dinner. Our lives have been engrained with our parents, especially after welcoming kids. It was how Raff and I had both grown up, with our grandparents always around. Our door was always open for Ma, Pop Pop and Nonna - Sofia and Layla loved every moment of it.

I couldn't bear the thought of telling them they had lost one of them.

Raff said he would come to the hospital to be with us, and my brother-in-law soon followed. We started reaching out to family members to let them know what was going on. We hadn't shared much before that, but now it felt important to prepare them for what we thought would be worse news.

The five of us camped out, between tears and silence, for hours in that waiting room.

From then on that night, every time a doctor walked by, I expected them to walk in and tell us something horrible had happened, but usually it was just a "status quo" update. Occasionally they would let us in the room, each time seeing her on more machines, tubes and medicines and the ICU nurse working feverishly. I asked mom to keep fighting and she nodded her head, still inside there somewhere, an encouraging moment. But each time I clicked the silver button that let us into ICU; I braced myself for what we would learn. Time seemed to move so slowly. We played Beatles songs for her and scratched encouraging notes on the backs of pieces of paper to hang on the walls around her bed. We tried to sleep on tiny wooden loveseats and even a yoga mat retrieved from my car.

At some point, the sun peeked through the tiny window in the waiting room. Morning came and my mom was still alive.

Hour by hour we saw tiny improvements -- glimmers of hope. The doctors started talking about more long-term recovery rather than just getting through the day. On day three, we finally were able to feel some confidence that she would make it. Her recovery continued and after a week she was able to come off the breathing tube and out of her medically induced coma. Doctors were using her case as something to share with other doctors; they were shocked she had pulled through.

The strangest part of the experience was interacting with someone who had no idea what happened to them, while you are overwhelming them with joy that they survived. My mom was confused and at times frustrated that this incident took her progress many steps backward. We were grateful she was alive, but all she saw was a mountain to climb. But we supported her forging on and she continued to heal.

Those next few weeks were hard, juggling life while my mom was in ICU. Feeling torn in multiple directions every day, wanting to be with her and home with my girls. But we got through it, one day at a time.

It took me a while to realize how traumatic those first forty-eight hours in the ICU were. They came out of nowhere and were a reality check that life can change in an instant. It took me months to be able to smell hand sanitizer without feeling overwhelming anxiety that would take me back to those days. But if you ask me what I remember from them, I would say much less about the hard parts and much more about the good parts. I remember her nurse, Ashley, telling us she was going to do everything she could as she furiously hung bags of fluid and IVs next to my mom's bed. She had kindness in her eyes and I believed she truly *would* do everything she could. I remember the doctors who would try to lighten the mood by cracking a quick joke or asking questions about my mom's personality so they could motivate us to keep the faith. I remember a woman walking into the waiting room in the early morning hours with three Starbucks lattes. "I heard you talking before and thought you might need these," she said. A total stranger, but she correctly guessed that coffee would be needed. I remember my brother-in-law trying to sleep on a two-seater wooden couch, probably the most uncomfortable sleep of his life, but it gave us a good laugh. I recall finally moving to a hotel the second night, and ordering a $36.00 6-pack of light beer from room service and then the three of us falling asleep before ever finishing them.

These are stories we would tell my mom someday, and she would roll her eyes and joke that we were "living it up" while she was in a coma. Coping the best way we knew how. Making memories in an ICU waiting room.

Unfortunately, what should be known about this time in our lives is that during this health crisis of my mom's, my mother-in-law Silvana was starting a decline in her journey with cancer, the beginning of which actually predated my mom's troubles. On the day my mom was released from ICU to a "step down" unit, Silvana was admitted to the same hospital for pain in her back. Subsequent tests confirmed it was tumors from her cancer spreading to her spine. Mere weeks after my mom's crisis, and the same day my mom was released to a rehabilitation facility, we were sitting in a different waiting room, while Silvana had surgery that she had a 50/50 chance of surviving. She did survive that ordeal, but the mountain to climb was even higher.

It would be almost unbelievable if I wasn't living it myself, but I would spend hours at that hospital (and subsequently the rehab facility they were both at) most days, moving between floors visiting each of my daughters' grandmothers. Each piece of good news for my mom was usually coupled with some bad news that Silvana was receiving, so it was often hard to keep my head above water. Wanting to celebrate, but facing other realities.

Our society expects that mother-in-laws are the burdensome part of marriage, but Silvana was not. She was the kind of person who immediately was your friend. I used to joke that everyone in New Jersey was her cousin, but that was because she treated everyone like family. She lived, laughed and loved with her whole heart and the only times she ever bothered me were the times when she would think less of herself, which was often. I wished she had given herself the love she so freely gave other people.

When my eldest, Sofia, was only 18 months old, in early 2013, Silvana was diagnosed with cancer of an unknown host. I point out Sofia's age because there was nothing that brought Silvana more joy than becoming a grandmother. She had waited to be a "Nonna" her whole adult life and she showered Sofia with an immense amount of love in those early days. It was gut wrenching to all of us when she found out she was sick.

One day, when Silvana was only a few weeks into this cancer diagnosis, she was visiting for dinner. As she watched Sofia sit in her high chair, I could see her get very quiet and start to cry. She didn't have to articulate her anguish-- I knew what she was thinking. This moment broke my heart into a million pieces because I knew what we all knew--how serious things were and the reality that she felt in that moment.

I accompanied Silvana to her first chemotherapy session one day in February 2013. The doctor sat with us first and went over the plan and the latest tests. He was cold and matter-of-fact. I wanted to see the good and find the hope but he was making it hard to do that. I couldn't wait to get out of his office. The chemo induction chairs were a breath of fresh air compared to that.

By the grace of God, a new doctor and some clinical trials, Silvana had three more years with Sofia, and subsequently Layla, but in spring of 2016 we started to see signs that time was not on our side. The surgery that she did survive that day in April left her virtually paralyzed. She was sent to a rehab center that would quickly send her back to the hospital. Deep down I knew what that meant. I knew she was too sick to have any hope of rehabbing in the traditional sense. Even after witnessing the miracle my mom had just gone through, and trying to keep a positive mindset, I had to face the reality that we were likely going to lose her sooner than we thought. I had to step into that "Strong One" role again because Raff was having a hard time accepting this fate. His mom was the most important person to him in the world and denial was, understandably, his defense mechanism.

Mother's Day 2016 was spent at two different medical centers visiting women on two very different paths with two very busy toddlers. It was probably one of the most stressful days, trying to make each mother feel special and celebrating them; one of whom was going through an intense recovery and the other who was, quite frankly, dying. My own Mother's Day was the last thing I was thinking about. Things still felt so unbelievable.

On June 11th of that year, we were woken up in the middle of the night to the phone ringing. My heart immediately started beating out of my chest as I could hear someone from the hospital suggesting Raff come because Silvana's blood pressure was dropping. He left immediately and I started trying to reach anyone who could come and stay with my sleeping girls so that I could go be with him. He called me back less than ten minutes later. "She's gone," he said. I will never forget the sound of his voice and the feeling that came over me. The reality that I knew was coming was so gut wrenching when it finally happened.

I was able to get to the hospital to be with him. On the way home from the hospital that day, I stopped by the rehab center my mom was still at to tell her in person. Silvana hadn't just been her daughter's mother-in-law, she was also her friend. I could barely get the words out before I collapsed into a hug with my mom. The stress of these last few months overflowed. My mom was here, but Raff's now was not.

Moving forward from the loss of Silvana was huge, but it brought Raff and I closer together as we navigated grief so large for the first time. It made us be more intentional about the time we were spending and making sure our girls felt supported to understand the loss of their Nonna. They were only four-and-a-half and two-and-a-half, but telling them was still the most diffi-cult explanation I had to mount to that point. It's one thing to grieve alone, it's another to grieve alongside your children, and this was the most painful part. As we often do, we turned to books to help them understand, reading through our own tears.

While I had lost my grandparents before, this was the first big loss in the sense that it seemed unfair. We were young, and we had so long to live without her. Death is so final. No matter how much you might understand that, when you lose someone this way the finality can overwhelm you. I learned that time does not heal, despite what we are told. Time can some days make it heavier, not lighter. Life without some-one gets more normal as time goes on, but the further and further you get away from them doesn't help you miss them any less. But the hardest part I found is that everyone moves on before you're personally ready. No one means to, but life simply moves on. The questions stop, the sympathy fades. You find yourself wanting to continue to talk about someone but you're not sure who wants to listen. Some days you want to sit with the grief and just be sad, and other days you want to push it away.

It took us a long time to take a deep breath from 2016. My sister got married that September and my mom was able to dance at her wedding, a really monumental moment that we all soaked in. In November, we took Sofia and Layla to Disney World in Florida using some funds we inherited from my mother-in-law. "A gift from Nonna," we told them. That trip was incredibly cathartic for Raff and I, getting to just have fun with our girls after they so patiently handled the changes of the past year. Silver lining, for sure.

Silver Linings:

- *I am grateful that I am able to step in during crisis situations and be strong for those who need it.*
- *I am grateful for the strength my mom had in those days in early April. She knew we needed her to be strong.*
- *I am grateful that my mother-in-law was someone who was so hard to lose.*
- *I am grateful that my mom was able to see my sister get married and enjoy her entire wedding.*
- *I am grateful for our family time in Disney, and thankful to Silvana for providing it for us.*

Chapter 5

Unexpectedly Lucky

"Two roads diverged in a wood, and I - I took the one less traveled by, and that has made all the difference."
— Robert Frost, The Road Not Taken

As we moved through the years after losing Silvana, we were able to find some incredibly happy times. We moved to a new town and settled the kids into new schools and made new friends. We welcomed Genevieve Silvana in August 2017, named after my great grandmother and the grandmother our daughter would not get to meet. We thought Genevieve would complete our family of five. My mom's health continued to have its ups and downs but we were all enjoying our time together. Early in 2018, my partner Kristin and I opened our yoga studio and it was an exciting time taking a new journey as an entrepreneur while still moving up in the corporate world.

I entered 2019 pretty excited. The year started with the birth of my niece and nephew--twins, quite literally on January 1st. Professionally, I was on an upswing. I was promoted to Vice President at the financial technology company I had been working for since 2008, one of only three women in that position in the company. My yoga studio was hitting its stride. I was feeling proud of myself as a mom of three girls, we were settled into our new house and community, and things were good.

Sometime that June, Raff and I were standing at a family member's graduation party, watching our girls play in the yard. For some reason, the conversation about whether we were done having kids or not came up between us. We were both pretty much caught in between "let's not complicate things" and "but one more might be fun." We both came from fairly small families and the dynamic of a larger family had always intrigued us. I distinctly remember the moment where I said "I just need a sign from the universe whether we should or not" and we moved on without talking about it again.

On July 26th, 2019, I dropped the kids off at school and went for my Friday treat, an acai bowl, full of way too much sugar, before working from home for the day. As I ate this indulgent breakfast, I started feeling nauseous with each bite. Confused, I pushed the bowl to the side and started working. A few minutes later, as the feeling continued, I felt the blood rush to my toes as I realized I knew this feeling very well. It was the same feeling I felt three times in my past when I was pregnant with my other girls. When it's your fourth pregnancy, you know. No, it can't be!

I drove to the store hoping to not run into anyone I knew and grabbed a pregnancy test. I knew those pink lines would be there, but when I actually saw them, thoughts flooded my brain. I have three kids, am a full time corporate Vice President, and a part time but kind of full time co-owner of a growing yoga studio. I was launching a yoga teacher training program in four months, drowning in mountains of home organization projects and had a to do list that only gets longer. I love babies, but having a fourth one wasn't totally in the plans at the moment.

I had asked for a sign and there it was, in two bright pink lines.

When I told Raff later that day, he admitted being overwhelmed with the same feelings.

There was no room in our someday-to-be-renovated home and no time in our life, yet as we looked at our three other girls, we still began to feel the excitement of another one just like them. We knew this surprise was a gift - a gift that some people long for. So we let our spinning heads tell our feet to move forward. The next two months were a range of emotions. Happiness at a new life, stress about the myriad impracticalities, guilt at the mixture of feelings. I barely wanted to tell people because I felt embarrassed. Who has four kids?! What kind of car do we need now? Will people even invite us anywhere anymore? How do you even fly with a family of 6?! Suddenly everything about our house was bothering us and everything felt overwhelming. We were arguing a lot and everything felt heavy.

When I was around ten weeks pregnant, I had an appointment with a psychic medium. I went to the appointment out of pure curiosity and a healthy amount of skepticism. As I sat there, giving no information about myself, a woman I imagine was my grandmother came through. Through the medium, she announced that I was having a fourth baby, and this baby was coming to teach me. I was blown away that she knew that I was pregnant, that I didn't think much about the other part. How prophetic that would wind up being.

Raff and I went to our first trimester screening at thirteen weeks, the same as we had done three times prior. We were still feeling a little overwhelmed but also excited to check this box and start telling people. This was always the appointment that made it feel safe to announce the pregnancy to the world, via social media of course. Right away, we saw a nice strong heartbeat which was a beautiful sight. But as the technician was scanning, I started to get a weird feeling that I kept brushing aside. She spent a lot of time measuring the neck and seemed to have nervous energy. She stopped with the small talk she had been making. She got her measurements, printed the pictures I asked for and said the doctor would be in soon. I didn't tell Raff about the energy I was sensing because I thought maybe I was imagining it. The doctor came in and was quiet, and immediately started measuring the same area. "The fluid in the neck is thick" she said, and I immediately knew what she meant. This was the measurement that always held importance in prior pregnancies, a measurement that flagged some genetic "abnormalities". My voice started breaking as I asked her what was next. She handed me a box of tissues and explained that we had three options:

1. get a chorionic villus sampling or "CVS" test right then and there

2. wait until week 18 and do an amniocentesis
3. Get probable, but not confirmed, information via a blood test.

After that, if we got a diagnosis, we could decide what to do, but "most people opt for termination," we were told.

Those words stung me so deeply. This baby that I was so conflicted about, so stressed about, suddenly he or she was all I wanted. I felt so protective of how this baby was being spoken about, like their life was suddenly expendable, nay disposable.

I am not a patient person, so we opted to do the CVS test immediately. I do not like unknowns, so thinking about waiting another 5-6 weeks, or the entire pregnancy, was not for me. I knew that carrying that stress for six more months wouldn't be good for anyone. I wanted to know what was going on so that I could prepare. I also knew that the CVS test could carry less of a risk of miscarriage than the amniocentesis, so it felt like the better option all around.

I tried to calm myself down, but when the doctor left the room my whole body started trembling. Raff and I were both stunned, our minds flooded with thoughts. I tucked away in my bag, the ultrasound pictures the doctor had printed.

They moved us into another room to perform the CVS test. Everyone was kind but serious, almost talking around me rather than to me. They told me that the test might be painful, but I felt mentally numb at that point and don't remember an ounce of pain. One of the technicians was monitoring the baby on an ultrasound during the test to help ensure that issues didn't crop up. I couldn't look at the screen. My fears allowed me to go to a place where I worried the baby had something that was not survivable. I was afraid to look at him or her in case I was never bringing them home. I was afraid to fall in love.

They told us we would hear something within a week and set us up with a follow up four weeks later. We left that appointment feeling like we were in a fog. I had to update the few people who knew about this appointment, mainly our immediate family. It was hard to have those conversations because there were so many unknowns. Everyone was trying to be positive that things would come back totally "normal," but deep down I knew it would be "something."

I slept the rest of that day away, mostly because I was required to stay in bed following the test, but also because I was in such a mental fog. Waking up the next day, I tried as best I could to put everything out of my mind. I barely thought about being pregnant, even though I could feel the baby kicking stronger and stronger with each day. I was scared to love this baby more, for fear of what unknown would be revealed.

If we did talk about the pregnancy, it was when we would google all the statistics about how a thick nuchal fold still resulted in a "normal" pregnancy. One article that Raff found talked about how boys can have a larger measurement naturally. Our measurement was only slightly above the normal range, so we thought maybe this was just that we were having a boy after three girls? We obsessed over every little bit of "hope" because we were fearful of what the test would find.

Six long days later, my phone rang while I was driving with my two oldest girls to a dentist appointment. I recognized the phone number right away as that of the genetic counselor's and my heart started racing. "Do you have a minute to talk about your results?" the voice on the other end asked. I didn't have a minute, but I couldn't wait to know. As I heard the kids singing along to the pop singer Lizzo in the back of the car, I figured now was as good a time as any.

"The test showed an extra chromosome 21 found across the cells which is consistent with Trisomy 21, or Down syndrome. Have you and your husband talked about what you would do in this situation?"

There it was. The baby has Down syndrome. I told her I needed to talk to my husband. I knew what she meant when she asked what we would do, but no, it was not something we had discussed. At no point over the past 6 days had we discussed that in any capacity. I pulled over and took her direct number and told her I would call her back. I took a deep breath and continued along to the dentist. I could have turned around and gone home, but I had already arranged many things to make this dental appointment work. I didn't want to call Raff while he was at work, it wouldn't have been right to give him such huge information while he was working with patients. I sat with the information for an hour, all the while smiling for my girls and alleviating their fears about the dentist. I think this hour helped me. I couldn't react. Real life went on and I had to absorb the rawness of the words. The baby has Down syndrome.

I realized that it was Wednesday and supposed to teach yoga that night. I texted my partner Kristin to ask if she could find me a sub for the class. "I just found out the baby has Down syndrome and I can't even think about teaching." She wrote me back in shock and that she would of course find someone. I didn't say anything else.

We finished up the dentist appointment, and as we got in the car, my OB called - the doctor who delivered all three of my children before that and had been such a huge part of my journeys. He had just gotten the report himself, and I could tell the information pained him. It wasn't what any of us were expecting. He told me he would see me on Monday for our next appointment and to call him if I needed anything. I numbly continued home.

Here I was. At a fork in the road. One way was the road less traveled. The other....the typical. I knew which direction I wanted to take immediately.

I'm remembering the poem by John Greenleaf Whittier; For all sad words of tongue and pen, the saddest are these, "it might have been." I knew I did not want to spend the rest of my life wondering. I knew in my heart that no matter what may lie ahead, I would never regret choosing to know this baby.

Raff was already home when I got there, so I pulled him aside and I said the words out loud for the first time "*the baby has Down syndrome*" and then cried the first tears. "I can't stop this baby's heart." were the next words that blurted out of my mouth. So blunt, but just what popped into my mind at that moment. "I know, I can't either," he said. I felt relieved. Fortunately we both said what the other one needed to hear - that in our hearts we had to give this baby a chance. In that quick moment of raw emotion I knew we were both "in" and that was all that mattered. I think about how things might have been if we weren't on the same page, and I am just so grateful we were.

I called my dad next, and cried as I told him the information. "We are still going to have the baby," I said. "I know you are. I know you are. That's my grandchild" he said, his voice cracking back. That sentiment continued as we told the other people who knew we were waiting for these results, and we had a team of supportive friends and family who were ready to help us figure this all out. "I don't know why I am crying," my sister said as we both knew this would be ok.

Later that night, I texted Kristin back, who I had left hanging with such a shocking text hours earlier, and said "We are still going to have the baby, if that wasn't clear. Just was in shock before."

"I knew you guys would be, and I'm so excited for you," she replied.

One of my best friends told me to reach out to a friend of hers, someone who grew up in my hometown but was a few years younger than me. She had a son with Down syndrome and my friend said we had to connect. I found her Facebook page and saw pictures of this beautiful, happy little boy and my heart immediately skipped a beat. Looking at his sweet face brought me so much joy. I messaged her, explaining who I was and said *"today we got a DS diagnosis for our baby and I've heard the word terminate more times than I can handle in the past week. It's not a choice we are making and at this point I just want to talk to someone and prepare myself to give this baby the best chance possible. Again, I'm sorry if this is out of line and if you're open to chatting any time I would appreciate it greatly."* I felt so strange sending that message. Basically, reaching out to a stranger with something so personal and deep.

She wrote me back soon after with the most overwhelming kindness anyone has ever shown me. She told me it would be okay and she validated the intense feelings she knew I was having without me even saying it. She ended her message with "your family just hit the extra chromosome lottery!" I believed every word that she said and knew that yes, it would be okay.

Yet, despite how much her reassuring words meant to me, despite all of the reassuring comments from friends and family, I cried myself to sleep that night.

The next morning, I woke up feeling like it was all a dream, and then it all came rushing back and the tears started up again. Yet I knew it was time to put one foot in front of the other. I called back the genetic counselor who I had spoken to the day before and told her that I was continuing my pregnancy. I could hear the twinge of surprise in her voice and she gave me some information on next steps, including reminding me that my risk of miscarriage was still very high. I asked for more information about Down syndrome and she said she could send me an article to read. An article that I quickly tucked away in a drawer after reading only a few pages because it seemed to only point out the thousand things that could go wrong for my child. It only seemed to add to my stress and worry.

For those first 48 hours, for lack of a better word, I grieved. On the other side of things now, it feels silly to say "grieve", but I think anytime there is an unexpected diagnosis, your mind has to shift from one idea to another. I grieved for the baby I had carried over the last 14 weeks and prepared for this new vision. I cried over what the unknown might change for our family and our girls. I had to feel those emotions to move forward, but of course they were mixed with guilt as I felt this sweet human life kicking away. I always wanted him or her; I just had to work through these feelings. I unfortunately knew so little about Down syndrome. Would he or she be ok? Would they feel less than all their life? Would people treat him or her badly? Mama bear kicked in right away.

But, there is also a part of that grief that makes you wrack your brain for what you did wrong. I was thinking back over the last thirteen weeks and wondering if there was something I ate or that wine I had before I knew that got us to this point. Was it because I was in my late 30s? Was it the ingredients in those Cheez Doodles? It's impossible not to go there in your head. But my internet searches told me that Down syndrome is a completely random chromosomal difference that occurs, it's not hereditary or "caused" by anything. Like finding a four-leaf clover, I read in one article, an apt analogy I would come to appreciate.

After that initial "grieving" period I began to feel some excitement. I knew that the part that Raff and I didn't say when we went all in was that we knew we would be okay. We knew that we were chosen for a reason, we knew our family would be strong enough for this journey and we knew that we had the ability to give this baby absolutely any opportunity her sisters would get - not because of money or status, but because of our sheer will. Doors wouldn't be shut and roads wouldn't be closed because that's just not how we accept life's mysteries. I was ready. We were ready. You can't choose every path in life and I felt this was a beautiful one to walk. Suddenly grief felt like the least appropriate word.

Two days later, on a Friday, Raff and I left for a pre-planned trip for our ten-year anniversary. It wound up being the most perfectly timed trip for two people who just got much unexpected news. We were able to take this time away to talk through all of our emotions without our girls there to distract us. Most of those conversations were positive ones but some were about our fears - for the baby, for us, for our family as a whole. I think it's natural as humans to fear what you don't understand, and I certainly didn't understand much about Down syndrome at that point.

On the first day of our trip, we ran into a friend of mine unexpectedly (I guess that's the definition of "ran into"). She knew I was pregnant so she asked how I was feeling. "Well…" I said, and I knew she could tell by my tone that something was up. "The baby has Down syndrome," I said.

"Okay?!" she said in a tone that was almost like she was waiting for me to tell her the actual bad news.

I sort of stumbled over my words as I filled her in a little bit more and she gave me some words of encouragement. I honestly can't remember what she said because the way she said 'okay' just sort of shook me back into reality. What *WAS* the big deal? I didn't get a death sentence; I got a Down syndrome diagnosis. Unexpected news, but certainly not bad news.

So much perspective had shifted over these last couple weeks since that twelve week scan. From the realization that everything we were worried about before the diagnosis - the superficial stressors of having another child - didn't matter, to the humbling awareness we could not assume this diagnosis was something to pity ourselves about.

That Monday we drove back from our trip and straight to my appointment at my OB's office. These appointments, while always routine in the past, suddenly started to feel stressful. As the genetic counselor pointed out when we spoke on the phone, our Down syndrome diagnosis put us at a higher risk for miscarriage basically until birth, so I felt like I would hold my breath until I heard a Doppler heartbeat at each visit. Fortunately we heard it right away, and then my doctor walked us through what to expect as far as upcoming appointments and extra ultrasounds. He prepared us, (if there is such a thing) for the added stress that would be put on us for the entire pregnancy.

Once we were done with all of the logistics, I wanted to get to the good part. I knew he had the report that had the baby's gender and I wanted him to be the one to tell us. He had been the only medical professional so far who didn't ask me "what I wanted to do," because he gave me the space to let him know first. He made sure we definitely wanted to find out right then and there and then left the room to get the report.

It felt like he was gone for an hour but it was probably two minutes. It has never mattered to me the gender of any of our babies, but this time felt so... significant. Would we be getting several new learning curves by having a boy? I had all girls and so I felt like a girl mom expert. Would having a boy make things feel even more different? Would he be able to play sports and do typical boy things? Would having a fourth girl draw me to think about her path being more different than her sisters? Would she look nothing like her big sisters? I didn't have a preference; I just really needed this new piece of the puzzle.

My doctor walked back in the room with the paper in his hand. "Three girls at home, huh?" he said, with a smile starting to appear on his face. He probably didn't need to say another word. He chuckled as he looked at the paper one more time and said what I could already tell he was going to say "well, now you have four daughters, congratulations!" We all had a good laugh for the first time in a few weeks. Of course it was a girl. We apparently only have girls, so I should have known it would be a daughter. A daughter whose almond eyes I couldn't wait to set my own on. A little girl who I already loved with everything in my heart. A girl with three big sisters waiting for her, ready to do all the sister things that sisters do. In an instant, I imagined the four of them curled up together during a movie night and my heart felt so settled.

Finding out she was a girl helped me so much in terms of framing this journey because I started to get to know her. I thought about how Sofia, Layla and Genevieve could not be more different from each other, but that they all were strong, determined, smart and really, really funny. I knew that our new daughter's differences would only add to their beautiful characteristics and the melting pot that is our family dynamic. I knew I would want her to have every opportunity that her sisters have had. I knew I would want her to be able to dream as big as they could. I knew my role would be supporting her and helping her get there. She was the pilot, I was the co-pilot. I could not wait to start our journey together.

The next day, I went in to talk to the owners of the daycare that Genevieve attends. A few weeks before that, I had asked them to save us a spot in their infant room. Our school had gotten popular over the years and the infant room was waitlisted, so I told them before most people knew I was pregnant. But when I next entered the school, I told them about the baby's gender, but also about the diagnosis and that they no longer had to save a spot.

"But...why?" they asked.

"Because the baby has Down syndrome," I said, thinking maybe they hadn't heard me right.

"SO?" one of them replied, in the same tone my friend had used days before that when she said okay.

"I don't know; I assume I will need to find special care for her." I explained.

"But if there's no medical reason why she can't come here, I don't see why she can't come here. We'd be happy to have her."

I knew this had nothing to do with money or business. They had a waiting list a mile long of kids to fill their rooms. They just loved our family and wanted to be a part of another one of our girls' lives. I know now that it was ridiculous to automatically assume she couldn't go to a mainstream daycare for the first few years. But this was another one of those early moments that I really needed. The reminder that there would be people ready to accept our girl with all of her expected exigencies, not only seeing things that were different. Maybe life wasn't going to change as big as I thought it would. It started to feel possible that her path could include many things her sisters did.

The idea of what this little girl was all about, had started to form in the few short days. When I spent 12 weeks of pregnancy imagining this baby in a different way, suddenly she was everything she was supposed to be with everything I had learned over the course of two weeks. I couldn't imagine her in a different way. I knew she would teach our family so much. I knew she would soften our hearts and light up our souls. I knew that she would change the world, whether that is through one person or through many. I knew that I would never be the same again.

While all that may be true, there are still some things about her being a girl that were - and are - hard for me to think about. I know that the chances of her having a biological child are extremely slim. I know that she might not marry or buy a house and have some of those traditional experiences—or will she?

Whenever I think about this however, I give myself a little reality check that there's nothing that guarantees any of my girls will do any of those things. Any one of my girls might not become a mother - either by choice or circumstance. They might choose not to marry and choose to travel the world rather than settling down in one place. It is my own ableist mentality that has let me believe that these traditional things directly correlate to someone's happiness or value. How could I assume that because my daughter with Down syndrome might not do these things that her life would be any less fulfilling? She might be the world's best Aunt to her sisters' kids or spend her life saving animals. Maybe she will find the perfect partner or maybe she will be content on her own. Like with her sisters, I can't predict what she will do.

Above all, I remind myself that it's not just in the simple, the mundane or the ordinary where we find life's beauty. The most special parts of life are when we break the mold, go against the grain and live a life that's anything *but* ordinary.

Suddenly the possibilities seemed endless rather than limited.

Silver Linings:

— I am grateful that Raff and I were equally committed to giving our daughter a chance when we got her diagnosis.

— I am grateful for my Dad's words that night, my first call to family after our path was clear, a reminder that our family would be behind us.

— I am grateful to my friend and our daycare owners for being among the first to let me know that this was "no big deal."

— I am grateful to my long time OB for being a kind voice throughout my pregnancy.

— I am grateful that I was able to so quickly start falling in love with my daughter.

Chapter 6

Acceptance

A few weeks after learning the baby's diagnosis, I still hadn't told many people. It was one thing to accept everything myself and another thing to be ready to tell the world. I still had my moments of feeling really overwhelmed, but they were mixed with joy and excitement. I remained very, very nervous about miscarrying this baby that I loved so deeply, that it felt safer to keep things to myself a little longer. I used this time to learn a little more about Down syndrome and the Down syndrome community. I wanted to be ready with some answers to questions that I was sure would come when more people were made aware. Some things were hard to read, like books or articles that were outdated or overly medical. Some articles I would start to read and then toss in the garbage because I didn't feel ready. At the advice of a friend in the community, I stopped reading these things altogether. No one hands you articles or pamphlets when you are expecting a typical child, detailing all of the things that could happen to your child throughout life. No one tells you their chances of developing cancer, autism, learning disabilities, etc. So these statistics felt like unnecessary stressors for a pregnancy that had enough stress on it.

When I felt ready, I turned to social media. Part of me was afraid of what I would find, but I now wish it had been my first stop. There are many ways that social media can get a bad reputation, but in this instance, it opened me up to a world I was hoping to find. Instagram showed me family after family who were raising a child with Down syndrome and thriving. I saw kids with Down syndrome doing the same things that my own kids did. I saw adults with Down syndrome doing both incredible and also very ordinary things. Suddenly the stereotypes and outdated statistics in those articles were replaced by reality. The reality that individuals with Down syndrome can live happy, fulfilling lives. The reality that my daughter's life, with the positivity that I was gaining exponentially, could be a great one.

Because of social media, I stumbled upon a book called *Bloom*, written by a *New York Times* best-selling author named Kelle Hampton. Kelle had a daughter named Nella who happened to have Down syndrome. When I found Kelle and Nella, I discovered a mom, daughter and family who appeared to be so...typical! They were taking vacations, having adventures, going to school. So ordinary in an extraordinary way. While social media doesn't show all parts of someone's life, the joy that Nella brought to their life was clear. I ordered the book on Amazon and took it with me to a two-day Jury Duty assignment in late October.

The book is about Nella's birth diagnosis of Down syndrome, and I found myself reading so many of the words I had been feeling. The shock at the diagnosis. Grief at letting go of the child you thought you were having. Tears for the bittersweet feelings of both sadness and happiness. Fear for all the unknown parts of the journey; worries for the siblings--it was all there. I devoured each page hoping to find what I was looking for - hope. I found it on page 87, in black and white:

> *"My sister told me she wished I could see what she saw - because what she saw was wonderful. She said I was lucky - that I'd been offered a shortcut to what life is all about when some people search for it their whole lives and never know. She said I had a*

secret - a secret to happiness and that, while people may look at me and pity me, in time I'd feel like I knew something they didn't. 'Someday, Kas,' she said, 'you'll feel so happy in spite of their pity glances. And you'll wish so badly you could let them know - that you could show them what life is about.'"

There it was. Tears streamed down my face in a quiet room full of strangers in that courthouse in Newark, New Jersey. For the first time, they were tears of joy. I hadn't even met my daughter yet and I knew she was going to change my life in a big way. I knew she was going to give me purpose in a way I wouldn't have had otherwise. I knew she would make me a better mom to all of my girls. I knew our family was going to be okay, probably more than okay. We were getting let in on the secret of life. We were joining the lucky few.

I immediately felt inspired, so I opened my iPhone Notes and wrote what would become my social media announcement about our news.

"Our family got a surprise earlier this summer that we would be growing by one more! Our emotions fluctuated between overjoyed and 'are we crazy?!' Then, about a month ago, at the start of Down Syndrome Awareness

Month, we learned that the baby who is coming will have one more chromosome than the rest of us.

A little girl who has already changed our world for the better and has already proven to find a way to stand out in a family with three older sisters!

We don't make boys and we don't turn down opportunities to make more space in our hearts, even when the path is a brand new journey for us. With open hearts we are ready for this next chapter, fears and all.

So for now, we are asking for prayers and good vibes that she will be a strong, healthy little girl. We are already so proud to be her parents and sisters."

Every word I said was how I truly felt and I suddenly couldn't wait to tell everyone. I wanted to frame the narrative so that the "I'm sorry"s could be silenced. I didn't want pity, I just wanted everyone to know how very wanted this little girl was; and invite them to join in our excitement.

Ultimately hitting "post" on the announcement a few days later felt like a huge weight had been lifted. I had spent since nearly the end of July being secretive in some way. Wearing baggy clothes. Finding reasons why I wasn't having a glass of wine. Pretending I was fine when I had a lot of stress on the inside. It was all out there now. I took a deep breath, and almost immediately started seeing responses. It was all so joyful. My phone was flooded with texts and Facebook messages wishing us well and congratulating us on this journey. Lifting us up and reminding us why we were lucky to be here. This baby was already so loved and prayed for and it felt like the celebration she finally deserved.

Silver Linings:

— I am grateful to those who have shared their lives on social media, to give hope to those who have come next.

— I am grateful to have found the book *Bloom*. It changed the way I looked at everything.

— I am grateful to have found the courage to tell the world about our daughter in a way that portrayed our joy. It has made all the difference in how our story was received and supported.

— I am grateful for the outpouring of love and support we received for our daughter. It helped shift a heavy time to one of celebration.

Chapter 7

The Pregnancy

Regardless of the joy we were feeling joining the lucky few, being of "advanced maternal age" (when did late 30s become geriatric?) and getting a Down syndrome diagnosis immediately thrust me into a world of "high risk pregnancy" status. I spent virtually every week at an appointment - a foreshadowing to raising a child with a disability perhaps.

At week 16, I headed into the first one of many extra anatomy scans, but this time alone. Since we booked the appointment during the emotional haze right after my CVS test weeks earlier, as luck would have it, we made it for when Raff would be on a flight to a business conference. I couldn't change the appointment and while there were many people I could have asked to go with me, I naively thought I had been through enough at the prior appointment, and thus hardened, that this would be tolerable; quick and easy.

I started to realize I had underestimated things when I walked into the waiting room at the perinatologists' office. The last time I had been there we were walking out knowing something was "wrong" with the baby and suddenly all those feelings rushed back. This place now induced such stress for me. Luckily they called me without a lot of waiting and we got started with the ultrasound. There was my girl – I studied her so much this time, now knowing her so much more than the last time. She was sitting cross legged and moving just enough to make the scan tough but make me chuckle. She was feisty already and I loved it. The technician was so kind but I immediately knew something was wrong when she got silent when looking at the heart. I endured this silence once before; it was the silence right before they told us something was "wrong." Like the last time, she finished her measurements and said the doctor would be in shortly.

The time between the scan and when the doctor came to discuss the results felt like a hundred years. The excitement and joy I had built up now felt like it was hanging in the balance of her life once again. When he did come in, he also was quiet as he studied some things himself. Eventually he got to the point. I learned our baby has a hole in her AV (atrioventricular) canal, an opening between all four chambers of the heart. While some holes have hope of closing on their own, this kind would require open heart surgery to close it. This news, although hard to hear, was not tremendously shocking. Babies with Down syndrome have a high risk of having a heart defect, ranging from very mild to very complex. I had prayed for the health of her heart, but prepared myself to hear what 50% of parents in the Down syndrome community must accept.

Luckily everything else on the baby looked great and they referred me to a pediatric cardiologist to get more information. The doctor asked me if I had any questions. Of course I had a thousand, but the only question I could muster was asking how babies typically do with surgery. "Well, most babies do well, but, you know, this baby does have Down syndrome." he responded, as if that made her weaker by default. He also reminded me with very little sugar coating that I had until 22 weeks to "change my mind," without directly saying what he meant. Immediately I sort of shut down and said I would follow up with the cardiologist. This was the first time I realized what I was up against. I do not mean up against Trisomy 21 or a heart defect. Those things I could handle. But in that moment I realized I would spend the rest of my life defending the fact that I believed in my daughter.

When I tell people how much we knew early on in this pregnancy, I believe there is an element of shock that we didn't take the "easy way out." Week after week of my pregnancy I felt that many doctors were shocked we were moving on. To Raff and I, this wasn't a choice. Our daughter deserved a chance and we were going to give it to her.

A couple weeks later, we went together to the pediatric cardiologist. To say we were nervous about this appointment would have been an understatement. All we knew up until that point was that our baby had a hole in her heart, yet we knew that could mean many different things. We knew there were things that could even impact her chance at survival. So this felt like the most anxious of all of the appointments thus far. Of all the things we learned about our baby, through all of the emotions of coming to terms with the diagnosis, what never wavered was wanting so badly for her to live.

In the office, the doctor performed a fetal echocardiogram, something that will always be incredible for me to think about. Being able to see the inner workings of a tiny little heart inside a tiny little baby inside their mama is mind blowing. He walked us through each area of the anatomy of her heart, explaining to us what we would be looking for over the duration of my pregnancy. He confirmed that she did have an AV Canal defect, which means that during development, the four chambers did not fuse together at the center. After she was born, blood would start to flow through that hole and apply pressure on the heart, leading to long term issues if not repaired. It was not the type of hole that would close on its own, so she would definitely need open heart surgery in infancy. The positive news, we learned, was that so far the left and right side of her heart were growing balanced, something that was good for the complexity of her surgery and her chances of thriving immediately after birth. This would be one of the main indicators we would track for the next few months.

The ironic thing? (did I hear you say you wanted irony?) He told us that statistically, babies with Down syndrome actually do very well with this type of surgery. That extra chromosome can often be a protective one. Two weeks before, the perinatologist had insinuated that Down syndrome would negatively impact her success outcome. Here we were, finally getting hope.

"I'm glad you came to see me. Most people don't get this far," our cardiologist said softly. I knew what he meant. I told him we wanted to give our daughter a chance, and he proceeded to tell us about the many children with Down syndrome that have been in his care with successful surgeries and now thriving. He told us that twenty-eight years earlier, he had been among a team of doctors that would take on the case of a girl with Down syndrome who needed the same surgery as our daughter. This particular girl had been turned away at many hospitals and came from upstate New York to New York City to successfully have her heart repaired. To this day, she drives all the way down for an annual checkup with him. She is a healthy, thriving adult with no lingering cardiac issues.

That story sunk in with me so deeply. I felt grateful to be connected with this doctor who believed in this woman back when no one would. I felt incredibly fortunate that our daughter would be born in a time where this wouldn't be questioned, and when something like this was fairly "routine." And I thought of all the families who were told no and didn't have the means to travel around until they got a "yes." Such an incredible disservice to many very worthy lives.

Focusing back on our daughter, the plan, our doctor said, would be that she would have surgery around three months of age. He explained that she would spend some time in the NICU after she was born until she was feeding well. In-utero her heart worked just perfectly, but after birth the hole can cause lung and feeding issues. Our goal would be to take her home and help her grow to around ten pounds, when she would be strong enough for surgery. If things continued as they were, with her heart growing balanced, I could deliver at the same hospital where I delivered my other girls. If things seemed like they might be complicated, I would have to deliver in New York City and her surgery would be much sooner.

This appointment wound up being the first one in weeks that I didn't cry in the car afterwards. Yes, hearing she would require open heart surgery when she was an infant was a hard pill to swallow, but our new cardiologist gave us something that day - hope. It was the first time we truly felt positive and supported in any of these intense appointments. He spoke to us directly about risks and complications but not negatively. He was medical but human. A breath of fresh air in this process.

As we started to tell people about this new news, everyone would wince and be surprised that we were at peace with it all. Almost as if this suddenly should have pushed things over the edge. Down syndrome was one thing, but a heart defect now surely made it too much, right? But honestly, there was nothing we could do about it and we were committed to giving our daughter a chance. We chose to see beyond the surgery and felt very fortunate that her heart issue is completely fixable and not likely to have long-term effects. We felt grateful to have been connected to the cardiologist and have access in our geographical area, to some great hospitals. Most importantly, we felt that we had a plan that would give our daughter the best chance at a long and healthy life.

As grateful as we were and as much as we were putting things into perspective, this pregnancy was really hard. I felt like I was continually pretending that things weren't bothering me. It was grating to hear "oh I'm so sorry" every time I told someone about her diagnosis. I felt like I was holding people's hands through my own news. I felt like I was making people feel better about something I was going through. Others would avoid the topic completely, maybe for fear of not knowing what to say or maybe thinking they were bringing up a topic we were uncomfortable with. I get it, but it still made for some awkward moments. Don't get me wrong, most people meant well, and I myself might have been one to say "I'm sorry" before I was having a child with Down syndrome. I didn't know better. But hearing so many "sorrys" about a baby that you're really excited about having is a very strange way to spend a pregnancy.

Aside from the boilerplate well-meaning comments, I felt like I had to stay focused at every doctor's appointment. I had to focus on my daughter when she was talked about like she was just a bunch of facts and statistics. Which I understood-- to an extent. I know the medical community needs to be transparent and needs to ensure people have a range of information. But that doesn't mean it's in the best interests of the mother's mental health to hear that over and over again. Even up until the very end of my pregnancy, I felt like I was defending my decision to have her at all. I felt like she was only ever treated like a Trisomy 21 baby and not a baby with Trisomy 21. I was worried this would be the case for her entire life.

Was I completely at ease every day with expecting a baby with Down syndrome? Definitely not. I had worries and fears and times where it felt like this journey would be overwhelming. But never once did I not accept my daughter and this path we were put on. I know there are many ways people react to this information and that is okay. There are people who do have a hard time accepting it and that doesn't mean they love their child any less. There are people who have the diagnosis delivered in more traumatic ways than I did. There are people who never even flinch at the diagnosis. We all love our children; we all will go to the ends of the earth for them. How we get there is irrelevant.

As my pregnancy continued on, we had fetal echo-cardiograms every three weeks, mixed in with growth scans and regular OB appointments. All of these things were necessary to ensure the heart was growing well and that there were no other complications cropping up. We were always looking for her heart to stay balanced, so I would hang on the doctor's every measurement. I was hoping to be able to keep my original birth plan of delivering at our local hospital where I had delivered our other babies. As previously stated, if things got more complicated, that plan would be moved to where they could handle a surgery on a newborn.

When her due date got closer, I had such conflicted feelings. For my previous babies, giving birth was the grand prize – finally meeting my girls after 9 months of pregnancy. I couldn't wait to see their faces and at the same time be done with pregnancy. I struggled a bit this time because although I could not wait to meet this beautiful baby, I knew that birth would be the start of her struggles with her heart. In-utero, the hole in her heart had little effect. When a typical baby is born and starts breathing, the blood starts pumping through the heart. When babies with a hole like Rhea's are born, blood flows too quickly through that hole and puts pressure on the lungs. Most babies need oxygen to stabilize this after birth and sometimes longer. Therefore, I knew that the usual post-birth experiences would be much different this time. I knew she would have a NICU stay and that her sisters likely couldn't meet her right away. This was of course before I knew that the COVID-19 Pandemic would wind up changing things even more.

I was choosing to stay positive throughout my entire pregnancy but I also knew there were realities I couldn't ignore. Being prepared was a huge gift both medically and mentally, but it also came with some burden to carry. I worried about so many things that sometimes feel silly now, but when one is delivered a diagnosis so intensely, like termination is the only way out, it's almost impossible for things to not feel so dramatic. I thought our lives would be changing in such monumental ways. I thought our family would become stamped with this label of "Special Needs Family." I thought I would lose any ability to maintain self-care for myself in ways I knew my mental health needed. I thought I would have a hard time to continue nurturing my three older girls in the ways they needed while caring for a child who would have a disability her whole life.

As I thought about these things, I also remembered that there were no safeguards against the hard parts of parenthood. There is no prenatal test for a lot of disabilities. There is no way to know if your neurotypical child might have a learning disability or face health hardships, for example. So I tried to keep the perspective. While I knew these things were more possible with this baby than with my other girls, I had chosen to be a mom. Deciding to have children meant taking the good with the bad, the ups with the downs and doing your best to lead with love. I couldn't say that one thing was just too much all of a sudden and I was out. That's not how it works. So whether our daughter had Down syndrome, a heart defect or whatever other things, she was my daughter—and she needed me! I truly believed that this little girl was sent to us to bring us more joy than we could ever imagine. This journey will be mixed with both tough and beautiful lessons we will grow from. The good times will far outweigh the hard times - I knew that in my heart then and I held that through the times when fears cropped up. I still hold that through the worry and stress, even to this day.

So while I was nervous about her impending birth, I was okay. In fact, more than okay. My stomach did little flips when I thought about seeing her sweet face. I could not wait to get to know her and watch her integrate with our now big crazy family. Learning she was going to be "different" and the challenges we faced on this road, have only made us fall more in love with her.

Silver Linings:

- I am grateful that my daughter's heart is fixable and that she has the chance at a long and healthy life.
- I am grateful to have been referred to the pediatric cardiologist we were, who guided us through this journey in a very patient and caring way.
- I am grateful for the parents of decades past, who fought for life saving surgeries for the kids with disabilities and helped the medical community understand that their children were worthy of thriving.
- I am grateful that I was able to keep things in perspective during this time and not stress an unhealthy amount.

Chapter 8

A Warm Welcome

In November of 2019, just a month after our Down syndrome diagnosis, I headed off to a business conference with my friend Carley to Charleston, South Carolina. This trip was planned well before I was pregnant, but I was determined to still go amongst everything that was going on. One of my misconceptions about this new journey was that I would have to let go of a lot of dreams and expectations as I became a "special needs mother," so it felt important to not miss this first thing I was doing for myself since getting her diagnosis.

I went on this trip to learn more about entrepreneurship and get some ideas to help grow my yoga studio. What I learned was so much more.

As Carley and I were sitting there on her first day, she grabbed my arm and nudged my attention to the last row of the VIP section. Sitting there was a woman with Down syndrome, taking in all the knowledge of the conference.

I learned, thanks to social media once again, that this woman was a self-advocate, Instagram influencer and barista at Bitty & Beaus Coffee Shop in Charleston. Bitty & Beaus employs and supports individuals with disabilities and she was one of their best baristas. As I scoured her Instagram page, I learned that she was at the conference because she was starting her own business.

My entrepreneur heart was singing. I knew I had to meet her.

During one of the breaks that morning, I mustered up the courage to go and talk to her. She would officially be the first adult with Down syndrome that I had met in my own adult life, so this felt huge. I had no idea then what the "right" thing to say was, so I spoke from the heart.

"My name is Taryn, I saw you sitting here and I wanted to tell you that I am expecting a baby who has something in common with you."

The woman sitting next to her, who I learned was her mother, leaned over with perked up ears and asked me to repeat myself.

I put my hand on my belly and said "the daughter I'm expecting has Down syndrome."

"WELCOME TO THE CLUB!" her mother exclaimed and gave me the warmest hug I could imagine.

I only got a few minutes with them before the conference resumed, but I knew I could probably go to dinner with these women and have conversation for hours. She told me about her new company and the best drink she made at Bitty & Beaus. Her mom asked me about the baby and her health in a way no one had yet. She didn't ask with her head tilted to the side in sympathy. She asked with pure care and joy. She was already in on the secret. She knew how good it was going to get.

Those few minutes were such a gift. Seeing her at this convention living her purpose just as I was reinforced that this journey was limitless. I wish it hadn't been a surprise to see her there, because she helped me learn that anything is possible for an individual with Down syndrome. It was just what I needed a few weeks into this diagnosis. I needed this woman's sunshine and her mother's hug.

That's the thing about the Down syndrome community. That extra chromosome is an instant family. There's an instant connection to people all over the world. Instant support. Instant encouragement. Instant love.

Silver Linings:

- I am grateful that I made the effort to take this trip and prove to myself that I could keep working towards dreams even with this new journey.
- I am grateful that this smart, beautiful woman was sitting there that first day, immediately teaching me so much about Down syndrome with her simple presence.
- I am grateful for my first official welcome to the Down syndrome community from her mother, whose joy towards my news spoke volumes.

Chapter 9

Our Sunshine

As I approached the final weeks of pregnancy, the COVID-19 pandemic was identified and becoming more aggressive. During that time I thought I would be nesting; getting ready for the baby and wrapping up the last couple weeks of work. Suddenly, the virus caused all the kids to remain home, doing some version of school. I was just trying to stay calm.

When week 39 got closer and the perinatologist discharged me from their care, my doctor and I picked an induction date around the baby's original due date. I had to be induced with each of my girls and never went into labor naturally. April 2nd would be her birthday and the countdown was now officially on.

In the early morning hours of March 29th, I woke up with some lower back pain. It took me a little while to realize that the pain was coming and going, and even longer to realize that I was in labor. Even though this was my fourth baby, this was a completely new experience.

At 3:46 AM I started logging the times of my contractions in my phone, realizing I was now in labor. I went downstairs and started gathering my things together, not even waking Raff yet, still thinking it could possibly be a false alarm. I put on *Will & Grace*, a comfort tv show for me, and tried to pass the time. By 5:26 AM I called the "on-call" doctor and walked him through my timeline. He suggested I head to the hospital as soon as possible, because fourth babies can come kind of fast. I woke up Raff and told him it was time.

Because we were two weeks into the pandemic, all of my middle-of-the-night plans to rush to the hospital with the help of neighbors went out the window. My dad was the only person we felt safe enough to come stay with the other kids, because he and my mom had been quarantined for weeks at this time. I tracked down my mom on the phone, who got dad out of bed and he quickly made the 15-minute drive to my house. We had been socially distancing to that point, but Dad and

I couldn't not give each other a hug as Raff and I left for this really eventful day.

As we drove to the hospital, I was upset that my OB wasn't going to be the one to deliver the baby. I had been sure he would treat this like any other time. I thought of all of the things that would be different; I had really wanted my doctor to be the one connection to the other times, but it was not to be. We got to the hospital around 7:30 AM and by now I was getting the full labor experience. After checking in, we walked into the Labor & Delivery room to start getting settled. On top of the warming table was a tiny little hat and a tiny little diaper. When Raff pointed them out, I couldn't do anything but cry. Seeing those items there reminded me that this tiny human who I loved so very much was coming any minute now, and I was desperately hoping she would be okay. I knew she was safe where she was, unsure if the outside world would be the same. Would she need oxygen? Would her lungs be okay? Would her heart work well? Would I be able to hold her before she's whisked off to the NICU? Would I only "see" Down syndrome when I looked at her? Would she be treated well?

I didn't have much time to obsess about these questions, because at 9:38 AM, Rhea Valentina Lagonigro was born. Quickly, and not-so-painlessly. She announced herself loudly, showing off her strong set of lungs thus immediately easing my fears. The nurse asked if I wanted to hold her, and I screamed "yes!" She placed Rhea on my chest and I started crying big, uncontrollable sobs, effectively soothing hers. I knew at that moment that we were going to be alright, because we had each other.

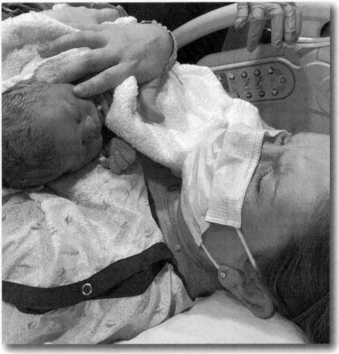

Holding Rhea after birth, a moment I didn't know if I would get.

In those first few minutes together, Down syndrome was the last thing I was thinking about. I didn't even look for any of the features I thought I would immediately see. As she had been since that day back in the previous July, she was my daughter, she was perfect and I was so glad she was here.

Rhea was taken to the NICU to be observed and I missed her immediately. We spent these nine very intense months together and I wanted her with me, but I was not surprised she had to go there. I had prepared for this, but it was still emotionally taxing. We made our phone calls to family and sent out texts letting everyone know she was here, taking this time apart to celebrate. A couple hours later, we were finally able to go and visit with her in the NICU. It was such a surreal feeling to see her connected to so many wires and in an incubator where we could barely touch her. I talked to her and stroked her hand, hoping she would know it was me who was there. Hoping she would feel safe and comforted.

Raff had to leave to get back to our girls at home and once he left he couldn't return per the new COVID protocols. I floated back between my room and the NICU, walking empty hospital floors, trying not to feel as alone as I felt. It was the most atypical stay of all my postpartum experiences.

It wouldn't be until later that night that I would be able to hold Rhea, which felt like a lifetime since I had held her that morning. I studied her face, thinking I would finally "see" Down syndrome. But I only saw Rhea. I had expected her to look so different, yet all I saw was the features she shared with each of the other girls. Sofia's coloring. Layla's lips. Genevieve's eyes. Such a beautiful and quite unexpected surprise.

Another surprise? I had stressed so much that I would come across doctors and nurses who treated Rhea differently. I am not one to jump to negative foreshadowing, but I expected what I had encountered during my pregnancy to continue. Yet here, with Rhea in the outside world, I only found kindness. Everyone told me how beautiful she was, how strong she was and how lucky I was to be her mama.

The next morning, I was standing at her incubator just quietly staring at her. I must have looked lost in my thoughts.

"She's going to be fine, you know," Rhea's NICU nurse said, like she knew I needed to hear that right then.

"She's strong, you'll see. Watch out for her," she added.

I nodded in agreement. "I know," I answered, afraid if I said more there would be a puddle of tears on the floor. Looking at this little baby, I was already so proud of her, and it took my breath away. I felt an overwhelming gratitude at how hard she was working to sustain life. She was my hero and she was only a couple of days old.

I was discharged from the hospital after two days and had to go home without Rhea, which was the hardest part of this experience thus far. My heart was in two places. I knew my girls needed me at home; but I wanted Rhea to feel my presence the same way my other girls had in those early days. We should have been snuggled up on the couch, her sleeping on my chest, not separated ten miles away.

Because of COVID, Raff and I had little help, and he was still attempting to keep his business open (before ultimately deciding to close for a month). I was home during the day, helping Sofia and Layla with virtual school, keeping Genevieve busy and hanging on updates from the NICU. Before and after Raff's work day, I would head to the hospital to drop off pumped milk and snuggle my girl. It was hard to close my eyes at night without her next to me.

As if she knew I wasn't doing well without her, Rhea quickly found her groove with eating and the hospital felt comfortable discharging her when she was four days old. My girl was coming home to meet her sisters, which was as special an encounter as I had imagined. We walked in the house, uncovered the car seat and heard a collective "Rhea!" like they had been waiting for her their whole lives. They flooded her with love just as I had expected, yet even more special.

Those first few weeks felt like more of a blur than the newborn stages I was used to with the previous three. With Covid precautions in place, she wasn't able to meet any of the people who had been so desperate to meet her. Immediate family met her from car windows and I tried to help everyone at home feel at ease with our reshaped world, while being completely sleep deprived.

At her first pediatrician checkup, we learned she had lost a few ounces since leaving the hospital. Because of her heart defect, her body had to work harder than normal just to survive, so Rhea needed fortified breast milk to be able to gain weight. I had to let go of the idea of nursing her and add a scoop of formula to pumped milk to make it high calorie. It felt like I was always either pumping or feeding her...in between helping two kids with virtual learning and keeping a two-year-old busy. I was probably the most exhausted I had ever been.

But, I have to say, this was a really joyful time in our lives. No, it was not the maternity leave I expected, but the silver lining of the lockdown was that my girls got to experience every moment with their sister. If things were "normal", Rhea would have been on the sidelines of sports and other activities, and our lives would have been preoccupied, to say the least. This time gave us an opportunity to slow down and ease into being a family of six, and soak up every special bonding moment together.

One night, we were feeding Rhea after another binge session of *Ozark,* a Netflix series. We always wind up diving into new tv shows when we have a newborn, and why we chose an extremely violent drug lord show this time makes me laugh. While snuggling her after she ate, I chuckled.

"What?" Raff asked.

"She's just a baby," I said and laughed a little more. It was at that moment that I finally had a chance to realize that the monumental change I thought was certain to happen the moment I welcomed a child with Down syndrome hadn't happened. Wasn't this child supposed to knock my whole world out of alignment? Rhea had all of the same needs as any other newborn, save for fortified breast milk and Lasix for her lung pressures. But she was just a baby.

I don't know what I had been expecting exactly, but I wasn't expecting things to be so...typical. Only a short time before that, multiple doctors had implied that terminating my pregnancy would be the better choice, yet here was this baby who was just like my other girls, with maybe a few extra needs than they required at that age. But, it wouldn't have mattered if she had a thousand more needs than they had. She is my daughter. I became her mama when I knew she was there. I fell even more in love with her with each new idiosyncrasy I learned about her, even the things that made me worry, or maybe especially so.

When Rhea was about six weeks old, we joined an online "virtual" group therapy session at a local school for kids with Down syndrome. This school is serendip-itously only five minutes from our house and is known for being an incredible and regionally recognized school for nurturing this extra chromosome. When I joined this session, I found for the first time the support that would only grow as time went on. Here was a place where Down syndrome was just a regular thing and it felt like a safe space to discuss all the worries and fears. It was a place where Down syndrome was celebrated, along with every little milestone that came with it. It was a place where these babies were instantly family, with cheerleaders for life.

Beyond that, I started to connect with other moms with new babies through *The Down Syndrome Diagnosis Network*, the largest national organization supporting new and expectant parents with a Down syndrome diagnosis. While it was beautiful to grow in this journey with people I knew my whole life, it was also pretty special to connect with other people in this new place I found myself. It isn't always easy for me to lean in to support from people, but this felt different. It was a joy to get to know this extended family we would now be a part of, knowing we would be rooting for each other's children for the rest of our lives.

Silver Linings:

- I am grateful for the birth experience I had with Rhea, it was a healthy and happy one.
- I am grateful I was able to hold Rhea immediately after birth, a moment (not guaranteed) that I will never forget.
- I am grateful for the NICU nurse who recognized Rhea's strength and shared that with me.
- I am grateful that Rhea's early days were nothing like I expected them to be.
- I am grateful for this new Down syndrome community that I am a part of and that it was so welcoming right away.

Chapter 10
Heart Surgery

Rhea, the name connoting a strong Greek goddess of the earth, and Valentina, meaning healthy and strong. We officially decided on our Rhea's name while walking out of the cardiologist's office in November 2019 while I was eighteen weeks pregnant. It was the visit where we confirmed that our baby would need open heart surgery in the early days of her life. Rhea was a name we tossed around after her Down syndrome diagnosis, because it felt so strong. As we walked through the doctor's office lobby, heads in a daze of information, I took Raff's hand and said "it has to be Rhea" and he nodded in agreement.

For the first two months of her life, Rhea was a baby with a heart defect. No matter how well she was doing, I knew in the back of my mind that we had surgery looming. In some ways, I was looking forward to it. After surgery, she would only have Down syndrome. Down syndrome felt easy compared to caring for a baby with a large hole in her heart. I was looking forward to getting on with the rest of our lives together.

While Rhea was much less "sick" than I had prepared myself for in those early days, that newborn phase was hard. She struggled to gain weight because her little body had to work so hard to compensate for her heart. We fought for each and every ounce of weight gain. I held my breath at every checkup until her vitals were read. Her breathing was faster than it should have been and her color was a little off. And of course, knowing she had a heart condition gave me an underlying worry day after day. I felt like I spent those months sleeping with one eye open as she lay in the bassinet next to me. But, she did develop well under the circumstances and by two months she was a happy, smiling baby. At one of her weekly cardiology checkups, it was decided that we should schedule surgery soon. She was starting to need more support from Lasix to maintain a safe lung pressure and had gained enough weight. Waiting any longer could be both unnecessary and harmful as her lungs could be impacted more and more. While we were hoping to make it to ten pounds, nine pounds two ounces felt close enough. It was time.

We did everything we could to prepare for our child to have open heart surgery. A friend whose daughter had several major surgeries told me to try to feel confident that you did everything you can to prepare, so that you can hand her off knowing you took her this far. You are surrendering her, yes, but are part of a calculated medical plan that got her to this point. We chose what we felt was the best hospital and had two meetings with a surgeon we felt was the best from his experience in this narrow field, a doctor who I will always be indebted to. Literally and figuratively a "giant" in the field of pediatric cardiac surgery, one of the tallest men I ever met, who would be operating on my daughter's walnut sized heart. I felt confident in him and therefore as ready as possible.

Before Rhea was born, we talked about many ways we would handle her open heart surgery. We had a line of friends ready to help with Sofia, Layla and Genevieve, plans for a meal train and had discussed ways for Raff and I to switch off hospital duties.

And then the COVID-19 pandemic hit, and it all went out the window.

Because this was June 2020, restrictions were at their highest at our New York City hospital and only one parent could be there for the entirety of her stay. That included both the day of surgery and for her recovery. We decided that it would be me, but this was an incredibly hard pill to swallow. My anxiety triggers are around health-related things, so I was worried about sitting there during her surgery alone all day and during her recovery. While that was hard to think about, knowing Raff did *not* get to do those things as her father was burdensome as well. It felt unfair for him to be shut out, but we accepted this and wanted to do what was best considering the times we were living in. This was so early in the pandemic that asking for an exception to the rule felt out of the question.

Among other things, the hospital also told us to prepare for up to a 14-day recovery period. Up until that point in motherhood, I hadn't been away from my girls for more than a few days, and here I would be leaving them during an incredibly scary time in the world, and taking their baby sister with me, from whom they hadn't spent a moment apart since she arrived home from the NICU. I knew Rhea needed me, but my heart was divided in two realms.

So, we went back to the drawing board, and enlisted some of our girls' favorite people to quarantine and help us out - my mom, my dad and my best friend Maura, who is also Rhea's godmother. All three quarantined to be able to safely come and go from our house. I knew they would not have a chance to miss me too much with this group standing in.

As the day approached, we talked to the girls about how Rhea was going to get her heart fixed and tried to prepare them as much as possible. We told them that we picked a really amazing doctor and they didn't have to worry, he was going to take good care of her. I didn't want them to be scared, so I answered their questions as realistically as possible, hoping they would have faith everything would be okay. Having to be strong for them helped me be strong for myself.

The day before surgery, I was changing Rhea when I fixated on her perfect little chest. In that moment, I couldn't see her rapid breathing or her pale coloring or the struggles to have her gain weight. I saw that perfect little chest and knew that the next day, it would gain a scar for the rest of her life. It wasn't really about the scar; I became overwhelmed with grief for what she had to go through and I wished more than anything to be able to take it away. I had spent so much time thinking about and preparing for this day that I hadn't really let myself sit with these thoughts and feel the enormity of this moment. Was that part of my defense mechanism? Maybe. But at that moment, I finally did. This was the first time in the many months since diagnosis that something felt unfair. This sweet little baby shouldn't have to endure such big things. I wanted to scoop her up and never let her go.

That night, I prepared the girls once more for the unknown amount of time I would be gone. They gave their sister a ton of kisses and helped me give her the pre-surgery bath and get her in bed. My mom came to sleep over because we had to leave at 5:00 in the morning to check in by 6:00am. Rhea was the first surgery of the day, which I was incredibly grateful for. The waiting was almost over.

I am sure it is no surprise that I didn't sleep a wink. I felt awful for that peacefully sleeping baby, knowing what was ahead of her. I knew deep down in my own heart that she would be okay, but I experienced such anguish that she had to go through it at all.

When morning arrived, we took her from the bassinet straight to the car seat, hoping she wouldn't wake up too much, since surgery, as with adults, precluded her from eating. During normal times, driving over the George Washington Bridge close to 6:00 in the morning would mean loads of traffic, but during COVID times, we flew right over, almost quicker than I was ready.

Once at the hospital, the plan was for me to bring Rhea up for "pre-op" and then come back down to get our luggage after I handed her off for surgery. Raff said his goodbyes to Rhea at the door and the emotions set in for me big time. I felt like I couldn't look him in the eye or I would crack. I knew how hard this was for him, and I knew I had to take it from here. Rhea and I went to the pre-op area where I got her changed into a tiny hospital gown (the most adorable part of the whole experience) and met with various doctors and nurses. Each one assured me she was in good hands. They all spoke to me with genuine care, while also making this whole day feel so straightforward. My beautiful, sweet girl slept in my arms during most of this time, as peaceful as ever, on the biggest day of her life thus far.

Eventually, it was time, and I had to hand her over. This was the part I had been most dreading. A true exercise of trust to hand over this most precious child to endure a serious but life-changing operation. She looked back at me with no clue as to what was about to happen and I did my best to stay strong and feel confident that she would be back with me in a short while. "You'll be okay," I said, praying that these words, while not understood by her, would be true.

I walked away from the room in a fog of my own thoughts. I couldn't tell you now if that hallway was busy or empty, because it felt like a quiet tunnel. A patient care coordinator stopped me and handed me her card and told me to reach out at any time with any questions. They showed me where to come back and wait and encouraged me to get something to eat. Rhea would be in the operating room for about six hours.

I stepped on to the elevator to go back and meet Raff and get my things, feeling very alone in that moment. What are you supposed to feel when you just handed off your daughter for open heart surgery? As if like clockwork, I started to get the first of many texts from friends, family and even strangers wearing yellow. I had made a casual suggestion the day before that our friends and family dress in yellow for Rhea (our sunshine!) and they started sending over pictures. I started feeling much less alone right away. I felt so lifted up by those simple acts that I was much more confident that it would be a beautiful, positive day. No one may ever know what those bursts of yellow did for me, right when I really needed it. It still brings me to tears to this day.

Back downstairs, I found Raff and we searched for food. Maybe a simple task in New York City most days, but during a pandemic, not so much. We found some danishes and bad coffee and Facetimed the girls back home, who were getting ready to start their virtual school day. We tried anything to distract ourselves from the fact that our daughter's open heart surgery was starting any minute.

Even though I would be sitting alone, I wanted to head back up to the waiting area quickly. I knew the team would come find me there with any updates, so I felt more comfortable being there. I wanted to be as close to Rhea as possible.

I sat down on the waiting room chair, smelling the familiar hand sanitizer smell I remembered from my mom's hospital stay many years before, tight through my facemask. For many hours, I sat there alone. I had armed myself with books and podcasts but had a hard time focusing. My sweet friends spent the day distracting me with texts, pictures, funny memes, anything. I tried to pump, but was so stressed that very little milk came out. I Facetimed with the girls and checked in on the school assignment app. I spoke to Raff often, who was waiting in the city, wandering from park bench to park bench. He couldn't drive back to New Jersey until he knew Rhea was ok. I barely noticed that lunchtime passed.

Just when I was starting to get extra anxious, at almost exactly the 6-hour mark, Rhea's tall, amazing surgeon appeared in the room. "Rhea is in recovery, everything went as expected." He gave me some other details but it felt like a blur.

Joy. Relief. Tears.

I called Raff and he answered the phone in anticipation. "She's out, all went well!" I could hear the relief in his voice change immediately. We both admitted we had been feeling more and more nervous as the 6-hour mark approached with no update, but didn't want to say it to each other as we talked. I called home and could hear the crack in my dad's voice as he could finally take a deep breath for the first time in days. He shouted out to everyone at my house this good news. More joy. A deep breath for the first time all day.

I knew very well that the hard stuff was not over, but I enjoyed this moment for a bit as I waited for them to let me see her. I knew this would be the second hardest part of my day, and I was not so patiently waiting to get it over with. I had handed off a peaceful and smiling little baby and knew I would now be seeing her sedated, with a breathing tube and connected to many other things. I also knew I might be seeing that scar I had now been dreading, however buoyed by the thought that all of this would help give her a long life.

After a while, someone came to get me and walked me to the Pediatric Cardiac Intensive Care Unit where we would be staying for her recovery. Our room was at the end of the entire unit, and walking by rooms and rooms of children with unknown (to me) heart conditions only added to the anticipation I had of seeing my girl. Whereas the surgical hallway felt like a tunnel only I was in, suddenly I couldn't help but absorb what may have been going on in each room I was passing. At the end of the hallway, I walked into Rhea's room and immediately searched for her through the machines and wires. There she was, sleeping peacefully, almost like the night before. After all of the mental preparation for this moment, I honestly felt peaceful. I could tell she was in no pain and there was nothing I saw that the doctors hadn't prepared me for. She was swollen from fluids so she looked like she doubled in weight since the morning. They had explained each tube and wire when we came for pre-op earlier that week, so nothing was truly a surprise. The nurse was rattling off numbers from the monitor that meant little to my layman's ears, but I could tell by the tone in her voice that everything was good so far.

In an example of how the human body amazes me, I suddenly had to pump very badly. After having not been able to for close to eight hours, it was like my body felt the same peace my mind did and was ready. Rhea couldn't eat yet, but she would have a lot of milk waiting for her.

As soon as I could, I Facetimed Raff so he could see his girl. We both told her how proud of her we were as she slept peacefully, unaware of the monumental task she had just completed. I stroked her head so she would maybe feel some familiar touch.

That first 24-hours after surgery Rhea slept the entire time but I don't think I closed my eyes for more than 30 minutes. There was constant monitoring and people coming in and out. Doctors and nurses rattling off stats that overwhelmed my tired brain. She ran a slight fever overnight which gave us all a good amount of stress, but it turned out to be nothing. I tried to sleep on my window bench with the most beautiful view of locked down New York City, the quietest I had ever seen it, but the perfect combination of adrenaline and stress kept me awake while my girl still peacefully slept next to me.

The next morning during rounds, we went over the plan for the day. Their goal was to start to prepare her to come off the breathing tube, and my goal was to hold my baby. But for now, I would have to wait while we gave her time to recover. It was such a strange day, because Rhea was still sedated. There was nothing I could do, so I passed the time with books, phone calls home and enough DoorDash food delivery service to keep someone full for a while. I took a short walk to Starbucks for some coffee and "fresh" New York City air after encouragement from our nurse that I step away. I got to take a shower and had plenty of time to pump.

Rhea's numbers continued to look good, so it was easy to relax a bit. Things started to get a little quieter and I was able to sleep a tiny bit more that next night, but I think any heart mom can always hear those late night beeps in her head.

I woke up on Day 3 feeling like this would be our day. And it was. Around lunchtime, they successfully removed her breathing tube and she was put on a CPAP machine as a step-down. I tried to play it cool until I not-so-casually asked to hold her. After a lot of maneuvering with tubes and wires, she was in my arms, and the true healing began for both of us. I started to feel the enormity of my gratitude to her for being so strong. If she was my hero in those early days of NICU, she was my superhero now.

I used this moment to take my first good peek at her incision. I am not one who is focused on cosmetic appearances, but this moment felt so huge. I thought I would feel sadness, but my heart swelled with pride. I was so proud of Rhea at that moment for what she just did. Here I had thought this scar would remind me of hard things, but it only showed me how strong she was, is and will be.

The next 24 hours were hard to witness because Rhea was off sedation yet had an uncomfortable CPAP mask on her face. We managed her pain but I knew she was ready to be tube free and couldn't get comfortable. I couldn't hold her for long periods or often because of the maneuvering of wires to be able to do so. But to my surprise, on day four we skipped a few steps and came off of all oxygen support! For the first time, I saw her new calm breath and beautiful color. We were so close to going to the step down unit, which meant even closer to going home. No tubes in our way meant we were able to snuggle (and even nurse!) a whole lot more.

At some point that day, they wheeled in an echocardiogram machine to get images of her newly repaired heart. I had been seeing her heart in this way since I was 18 weeks pregnant and first visited the pediatric cardiologist. Echo after echo every few weeks while pregnant and then weekly once she was born. My untrained eye knew every inch of this tiny little heart, so when the technician put the wand to Rhea's chest on this day, I started crying happy tears for the first time. It was fixed. The giant hole, it was gone. Sweet, sweet relief.

Five days after open heart surgery, I met with the doctors during morning rounds, expecting them to move us to the step down unit that day, but their words surprised me. "We think we are good for discharge."

What?!

They were happy with her numbers and her recovery so we were going HOME! I couldn't believe it. While it would still be a few hours for them to get the discharge together, I packed our stuff like they were going to change their mind. I had plenty of time to sit holding Rhea while I waited for our paperwork and for my dad to come pick us up.

I realized while snuggling with my sweet girl that I was wrong in how I felt about this surgery the whole time. I couldn't wait to put it behind us from the moment I learned surgery would be a fait accompli. But this experience would be something I would never leave in the rearview mirror, as it were. These days would always be with me. Rhea will always have been a heart baby, stronger than I have ever had to be. I will always be a heart mom, rooting for kids who come next in the way only a heart mom can understand. I will always have gratitude for this journey because it brought me to where I am today, a deeper connection to what is truly important. It brought me friendships with women who are some of the strongest I know. Above all, Rhea became my hero those days in June 2020 and I will always let her know that.

We both wear scars from this experience with pride, Rhea's on her chest and mine in my heart.

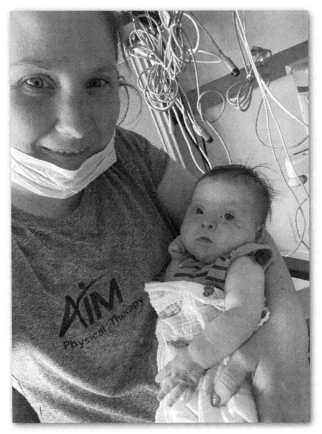

Rhea and I on the day of discharge.

Silver Linings:

— I am grateful that Rhea had a successful surgery and a textbook recovery.

- *I am grateful for Rhea's cardiologist, her surgeon and the surgical and nursing teams at Columbia University Medical Center in New York City, for repairing Rhea's heart and giving her the chance for a long and healthy life.*
- *I am grateful that my friends and family stepped in, mostly remotely, to lift us up on that day and make us feel much less alone.*
- *I am grateful that Raff and I were able to find the strength within us to confidently support our daughter through open heart surgery.*
- *I am grateful that Sofia, Layla and Genevieve were able to be strong while having their mama away and knowing their sister was going to have a major surgery. My other heros. They even welcomed us home with a giant homemade sign.*

Chapter 11

Just Down Syndrome

Recovered from heart surgery, we entered the next chapter, where Rhea only had Down syndrome and was no longer a baby with a broken heart. I had learned so much in the short time since her diagnosis and was ready to start a new path in our Down syndrome journey. We held off on standard early intervention therapies until about a month after her surgery, but started with Physical Therapy and ultimately Occupational Therapy and Speech Therapy. At first, I found our new routine a little overwhelming. These early therapies were in the "virtual" or online realm because of the pandemic, so it was all falling on me to become a quick study. I put so much pressure on myself as far as how much time we were spending working on things in between.

One day, one of our therapists listened to me talk about how much had just transpired the week before. I was feeling particularly overwhelmed that I barely thought about therapy in between sessions let alone officially practiced things. She said "don't worry, she has therapy without you even knowing it," referring to Rhea's three big sisters. Our house was so busy, but that busyness was actually a big part of Rhea's development. I felt such relief and was able to trust that Rhea would be fine - what I couldn't give her because I had three other kids, those three other kids were giving her just by playing and talking with her.

Rhea's therapies often feel like my own therapy sessions as well. Usually when I am feeling most over-whelmed, our therapists know just what to say and what encouragement to impart. They often make everything feel so "normal" in the moments things feel anything but.

The other beautiful thing that happened after surgery is that Rhea and I were able to start exclusively nursing. This had been something that I expected to never happen, from early on in my pregnancy. Even without Rhea's heart condition, I had been told that nursing would be a challenge because of the low muscle tone associated with her Down syndrome diagnosis.

Not wanting to hit every part of this journey with a "no," I started nursing her once a day among her fortified bottles pre-surgery. I knew that if we could establish a latch, we would ultimately have a chance at successful breastfeeding. This was not an ego thing. Maybe if Rhea was my first daughter, this wouldn't have been so important to me. Since I had the chance to nurse all three of my older girls until they were about a year old, I really wanted to have these moments with Rhea. Of all the things that were different because of NICU, heart defects, Down syndrome and COVID, this was something that would connect all four infant experiences together. I wanted to have that bond with her the way I had with my other girls.

A few weeks after surgery, when she was three months old and we were informed we could stop fortifying her milk, I started increasing the amount of nursing sessions. One day, she refused her bottles and only wanted to nurse. That nursing continued until she was 15-months old and decided she was done with nursing (mom wasn't quite ready!). But, we had a full year of nursing just as I had with my other girls. More importantly, it was the first time we busted a big myth that helped me to realize that this was OUR journey and no one else's. Likelihood does not equal guarantee. We weren't going to let statistics tell us what we could do.

As those months after surgery continued on, I found more lessons in trusting the process and trusting in what I call "Rhea time." Every time I felt frustrated or worried that we had been working on a milestone for so long, suddenly it would click: we learned that her development comes in "bursts." We will have a lull for a little while and then all of a sudden she will pick up a bunch of new things at once, either cognitively or physically. These moments come with such joy because they are never guaranteed. They feel like a gift that you've been waiting to unwrap each time while patiently waiting for it. It's been such a surprisingly beautiful way to live.

In late March, on the eve of Rhea's first birthday, I reflected back to a time just over a year before that. In February 2020, a mom of a teenage girl with Down syndrome met me for coffee after a mutual friend connected us. Our stories had so many similarities, including an open heart surgery for her daughter in infancy. During a time when I was still learning about Down syndrome, she gave me so much hope, telling me all about her daughter and just how life in general had been for them. One thing that she told me that stuck with me for that first year; she said that she remembered looking around at her daughter's first birthday and thinking that they were ok, and that they would be ok. She said they felt like just any other family and that they could do things like any other family—inspiring!

For a year, I held that affirmation in my heart as my silent wish, that on Rhea's first birthday, I would also look around and know that we were ok.

As I reflected on that day, March 28, 2021, one day before Rhea turned one, tears formed in my eyes. We were more than ok--so much more. We did it. We survived the NICU and those early days of cardiac issues and low weight gain. We survived open heart surgery at two months old, and during a global pandemic to boot. We reached for milestones and we attained them. We loved and laughed and smiled so much. We met new people who have become family. We are part of a community that is quite honestly a privilege to be in. I've gotten to know people who rock an extra chromosome who feel like heroes in my eyes. We've watched people we've loved our whole lives learn with us and shout Rhea's worth. We found our groove as a family of six.

I felt such relief even though I believed it all along. But it felt like I could finally feel confident in those words.

I was reminded of what I knew the moment I laid eyes on Rhea; that if I could go back and change the course of our future I simply wouldn't do it. If I could go back and remove one chromosome I wouldn't. Rhea was perfectly made. It is a privilege to be given the important gift of raising her, and I am so grateful for the opportunity.

As I woke up the morning that my last baby turned one, my heart could not have been fuller.

Silver Linings:

- I am grateful for the most patient therapists with whom I have gotten to share, laugh and grow.
- I am grateful for our breastfeeding journey, an unexpected reminder that we will forge our own path.
- I am grateful for all that was shared with me by the mom who has walked this path before. Her words were so important as Rhea's birth approached.
- I am grateful for the ultimate lesson in patience that comes from trusting your child to determining the pace of their journey. I love this version of motherhood.
- I am grateful, beyond measure, for Rhea, the 47th chromosome, and all of the blessings that raising a child like her.

Chapter 12

Sisterhood in the Lucky Few

One of my prevailing worries after finding out about the baby's diagnosis was for my other three girls. Raff and I were secure in our decision that WE could handle it, but we also have three other people who rely on us to do our best for them. My first thoughts were all of the negative things - I imagined people making fun of them for having a sister with a disability. I imagined how much of my time might be pulled away caring for her. I imagined her being a burden to them as they got older. I overall manifested this negative experience for them in those early days of knowing.

One day I stumbled upon an article about how adults with a sibling with Down syndrome actually reported that their lives were tremendously better because of it. It sort of hit me that morning - my kids would have an experience not many people get. They were actually becoming one of the lucky few. They will grow up not knowing much different, so maybe they will be less inclined to view differences in others as a negative thing, or something to be fearful of. They will learn patience and tolerance very naturally, in a way that we might not have otherwise been able to teach them. Having a sister with a disability may be quite normal to them, just as having an uncle with one was to me. Yes, I'm sure somewhere along the line someone will say something mean to them about it, but we will teach them to understand that if someone is going to say something purposefully mean about their sister, that's probably not someone whose opinion matters, nor are they worth one second of the time to be angry. None of that will be easy, to myself included, but life isn't guaranteed to be easy and I hope there will be many beautiful parts for them to feel grateful for.

My children will never be perfect and there will be stumbles along the way, but I wholeheartedly believe that their lives will be better with Rhea in it.

Very early after Rhea's diagnosis, we made the decision to be very open with our two oldest girls about their new sister. Genevieve was barely two years old at the time, but we wanted Sofia and Layla to understand this journey we were embarking on. Kids fear what they don't understand and they often fill our gaps with their own version of things. We didn't want to tiptoe around the word Down syndrome, or for them to feel for a second that there was something to be ashamed or afraid of. We wanted them to be able to ask questions and to be part of the learning experience. I was eager to know what they wanted to know because maybe it would help me navigate things myself. I wanted to prepare them for other things, like not being able to hold their newest sister as quickly as they did our last baby (they had already been fighting over who got to go first!). I knew there would be lots of other things different about those early days as she awaited heart surgery and I wanted them to feel comfortable asking questions. This was their journey as much as it was ours, and I wanted them to feel a part of it—as they certainly would be going forward.

I tracked down some age-appropriate books about Down syndrome and talked to them about their new sister. Raff and I explained that it might take their sister a little longer to do things they might take for granted and she might need some therapies to help her get there. I should have realized that they would have a very kid-appropriate reaction to the whole thing. Their reaction made me wish that was how we all approach things in life. Sofia said very matter of factly "well if it takes her longer to do things I'll just help her until she figures it out!" and Layla had more questions about the hospital than anything else. I knew there would be a lot more learning and questions to come, but at that moment they just couldn't wait to welcome their newest baby sister, and I felt such relief that we could talk about Down syndrome in such a positive way. I felt so fortunate to be welcoming our girl with these sisters already on the team.

While I never want the girls to feel an inordinate responsibility for their sister as she (and we) got older, it would be impossible to not think towards the future. I know they will each, as a matter of course, find their own roles in their sister's future. I'm glad there will be three of them to share whatever role they need, or will want, to play. We are raising our daughter to hopefully have as much independence as possible, but it is a comforting feeling knowing she has three big sisters with whom to experience the joys of life.

One day, long after her sister had arrived, Sofia asked me why we do certain things for Down syndrome. "Why do we talk about it and raise money?" she asked.

I thought about how to respond in an appropriate way, but honestly struggled with the right answer for a child. "Well, some people think that Down syndrome is a bad thing. So we speak up so that people understand that someone with Down syndrome should have all the same opportunities that anyone else has."

"Why would people think Down syndrome is a bad thing?" she asked, genuinely confused at that thought.

"Well, sometimes when people don't understand something, they think it's negative, so we just try to help everyone understand Down syndrome a little more, so they don't think Rhea is 'less than'" I answered.

"Okay," she said, her tone still trying to understand why anyone could possibly think anything about her sister wasn't wonderful.

Navigating my children through this journey has been such a humbling experience. Children don't see these differences as easily as [some, nay most] adults do. I worry that it will be shocking to them if and when someone does point out their sister's differences in a negative way, because they only see Rhea and don't know anything different. By necessity, they now spend more time in the Down syndrome and disability community. Much like how I grew up with my Uncle Robert, growing up with someone with a disability will become so "typical" to them. I'm excited to see how it shapes them.

Silver Linings:

- I am grateful that I quickly found the article about siblings with Down syndrome, as it calmed my anxious heart for my girls.
- I am grateful for the innocence and purity of young children's hearts and how much they have taught me about how we should love and respect others.
- I am grateful that my girls will grow up with their sister. I hope it will shape their lives in so many positive ways.

Chapter 13

Saying Goodbye

The COVID pandemic took so many things from us, but it helped to prioritize what was important. We made a decision early on that we were going to do everything we could to keep seeing my parents. My girls are incredibly close to their "Ma and Pop Pop" since we all live nearby, and keeping them all away from each other would have affected everyone's mental health in a way we weren't willing to risk. Every decision we made and safety measure we took was about keeping us all healthy and thus able to spend time together on a regular basis.

Christmas Day in our house is normally a huge celebration that we host for extended family. We've been hosting the holiday since we had our first home and it's my favorite day of the year. I love cooking for the large group and the warm feeling that Christmas provides.

Christmas 2020 was obviously a vastly different day. My sister was with her husband's family so it was just us at home with my Mom and Dad. As the day went on, I remember feeling deep down what a beautiful day it was. We had such great conversations that day, the girls got to stay in their pajamas and play with their toys and the food was still as decadent as always. It was one of those days I knew to appreciate while it was happening, for reasons I didn't understand yet.

In February of 2021 my mom called and told me that her doctor was concerned that her leukemia from two years ago was back and wanted to repeat blood work two weeks later. At first, I wasn't worried. My mom frequently got unsettling news or had little scares so it had become common to get calls like this. But sure enough, after checking again, and ultimately doing a bone marrow test, it was back. My initial reaction was "oh come on!" but I also had convinced myself at this point that my mom had nine lives and used only seven or so. Ironically, my mom seemed the healthiest she had been in a long time, so I felt like this would be another thing she could get through, and ultimately conquer.

Her doctor wanted her to quickly go into the hospital for treatment but she asked for a couple days to get things in order. She would be going in on Friday March 19th and would do inpatient treatment for up to ten days so that they could monitor her myriad health issues. We were all disappointed that she would miss our family's annual St Patrick's Day dinner that Saturday. It was a meal that she has made famous over the years, with our circle of family and friends growing in size yearly, to enjoy this once-a-year Irish feast. Because she would be in the hospital, and because of the pandemic, I would take on cooking the meal for just my family, my dad and my sister's family.

The night before my mom went into the hospital, I decided to follow her recipe for the first time to make a full corned beef and cabbage meal with Irish soda bread just for her. Part of me just didn't feel right about her not having the chance to enjoy the meal she looked forward to all year. Did I know what was to come? I'm not sure. But the girls and I drove dinner down to her house and spent an hour or so there. She held Rhea and we distracted ourselves from what she would start the next day. I snapped a picture of her and Rhea, another thing I did without knowing why. My mom hated pictures of herself, but something told me to capture the moment. We said goodbye, confident we would see her in ten days or so when treatment was over. She called me that night to tell me how much she loved the meal and that it was better than when she made it. "Well," I said, "you can take back the reins next year."

That was not how things went at all.

Her treatment started the next day and things seemed to be moving along well. She was feeling good and her biggest complaint was complete and utter boredom. Because she was on a cancer floor, COVID protocols wouldn't allow any visitors, so we relied heavily on Facetime to stay connected.

On March 27th, my mom Facetimed from the hospital to join in while we sang happy birthday to Rhea for our family's first birthday celebration. I remember how happy mom looked on that little screen. Again, another moment I didn't realize was resonating with me for a reason. The next day I was busy cleaning up from the celebration the day before, so the day passed and we didn't have a chance to speak. My dad and sister both had spoken with her and relayed to me the "status quo" updates. On Monday, Rhea's actual birthday, she didn't answer her phone and never reached out. I thought this was so strange that she didn't call because she had never missed one of the kids' birthdays. I even felt disappointed that she let the whole day go by without calling—not like her at all. What I didn't know was that she had slowly started slipping away. She completely stopped answering her phone, even though we were flooding her phone with calls and texts. Over those next few days we tried to get information as best we could from hospital staff, while not being allowed to visit. They assured us that she was resting and they were trying to figure out why she was so sleepy. While they did that, they pulled back on the cancer treatment temporarily, assuming that was the cause.

That Friday, Good Friday, the hospital called and told my dad he was allowed to visit, making an exception to the COVID rules. I knew this wasn't good, just like that time years ago when she had serious issues, the doctor told me to immediately call my dad. I stepped back into "The Strong One" role and reached out to my mom's oncologist and asked that he tell me what was going on. He explained that her body wasn't handling treatment well, so they had stopped it, yet she wasn't responding appropriately to that change. If they couldn't start up treatment again by the following Monday, we would likely be looking at hospice care.

Gut punch.

After my dad visited that day and spoke with the doctors, they moved her off the oncology unit to a step down unit in the interim. We were finally able to visit, but only one at a time, one person per day. While we were going through our worst, my dad, sister and I couldn't even be there all at once to support each other.

By that following Tuesday, we had to accept that hospice care was the path. My mom was still completely asleep, so when we each did visit, we played music and talked to her, just hoping that she could hear us.

The day after she was moved to hospice, in the early morning hours of April 7th, it was my turn to get the call from the same hospital Raff received about his mother five years prior. My mom passed away peacefully while sleeping. They had to call me because for the first time in any of her hospital stays, my dad had accidentally let his phone battery die. I had to be the one to call my dad and sister to let them know. I know this was no coincidence that it was set up to let me be "The Strong One" one more time.

In the days leading up to this, I knew it would be that day we would lose her. April 7th was five years to the day since we thought we would lose her the first time, that fateful night that they told us she needed a lot of luck. In some strange way, I knew that would be her sign that she was grateful for those five years. And a little bit of her humor one last time.

That day kicked off a journey with grief that I am still grappling with, and probably always will. Losing a parent makes everything feel incomplete in some way.

There's always a phone call you wish you could make, a seat that goes empty at the dinner table and a person always in your corner who is no longer there.

Grief catches you in little moments that you least expect. One day, two months after losing her, I was going through baby clothes to change over to summer. Out of the bin I pulled a baby's "onesie", a one piece garment that said "grandma's sweetie." My mom had given that to Sofia when she was young, and each girl wore it. It's a onesie that I wouldn't have thought so much about while she was among us. But Rhea would be the first of my girls to wear it without a grandmother. None of my girls would have a grandmother at their graduations or weddings. I knew that feeling all too well. The weight of grief felt so heavy.

I have learned when I encounter these moments of grief, it's best to lean into them. Oftentimes, I might play my mom's favorite music from The Beatles, listen, sing or cry. I might retrace moments from the last year, focusing on the good memories, but sometimes the most difficult ones. Sometimes I'll look out for signs that are always there, either a specific bird or a song coming on at just the right time. In some ways, I've never felt closer to my mom, because I think about her and feel her presence in such strong ways.

It would be easy to be angry that you lost your mom when you're only 39. It would be easy to be angry to have to tell your young children for the second time that they have lost a grandmother that was a best friend to them.

And I am angry to an extent. But as I knew my mom felt, those were five bonus years. If we had lost her the night we thought we would, she wouldn't have seen my sister get married. She wouldn't have met my two youngest daughters. She wouldn't have seen my sister become a mom and meet my niece and nephew. She wouldn't have had hundreds more date nights with my dad and celebrated many birthdays and holidays.

Anger has been replaced with gratitude that we had those moments. Wishing we had more time, of course, but trying to find happiness with the time we had.

In true alignment of sadness and comfort, my mom's brother Robert passed away on May 8th, 2021, one month after his beloved sister. It was such a shocking phone call to receive so close to losing my mom. My dad and I had been able to visit with him the week before and he seemed to be doing so well. But again, I knew this was no coincidence. He missed his sister and understood that she was gone. For their whole lives, she was always there for him in such an inspirational way. Together since the womb, they weren't meant to be apart. He wasn't meant to be without the woman who never left his side and I know she called him home to be with her.

> "Love you forever and forever.
> Love you with all my heart.
> Love you whenever we're together.
> Love you when we're apart."
> –Lennon/McCartney

Silver Linings:

— I am grateful for the Christmas that we had in 2020 and for the quality time that it afforded us with my mom.

— I am grateful that I knew to make my mom her St Patrick's Day dinner and bring the girls to see her. It was a sweet "last time."

— I am grateful that my mom got to sing happy birthday to her last grandchild, a memory I will always treasure.

— I am grateful that my dad's phone died that night, so that I could be the one to break the news to him and my sister, a familiar voice rather than a stranger.

— I am grateful that I am in tune with myself to sit with grief and let myself feel the emotions. It has helped me avoid bottling it up.

Taryn Lagonigro

—   I am grateful that both my mom and my Uncle Robert
    passed peacefully and together. It has been such a
    comforting feeling.

C h a p t e r   1 4

Going All In

On September 30th, 2021, I joined "The Great Resign." The COVID pandemic has shown us so much about how to live our lives, and I knew that no longer included Corporate America for me. I have been fortunate to work for a company that allowed me to be a mom. I say that with immense gratitude because I know that is not the case for so many women. I started there in April of 2008 as a 26-year-old single woman in a staff level position and I left as a married mother of four and one of the few female Vice Presidents in the company. I navigated through many roles there and was able to both successfully complete my work and successfully set my boundaries as far as work/life balance. I found that communicating these needs openly helped create trust with both my teams and supervisors over the years. I never missed a deadline yet I also never missed a school program.

Then a pandemic and a child with a disability showed me that I didn't want to do it all anymore. I learned from losing my mom that life is short, and you cannot wait forever to take a leap of faith. My job had provided for so much, but I didn't want to rush through life in that way for one more day. I wanted to find ways to create a life that was meant to live intentionally with my family, just like my dad had done when I was a child.

Am I working? Harder than ever. But for the first time it's on my terms, inside my own boundaries. It's scary and unknown but it's meaningful.

I have always felt like I was meant to do more with my life from a career perspective. For a while, when I was promoted to Vice President, I thought that was what it was. Maybe I was supposed to be the pioneer mom of four who can do it all in a male dominated industry. But I kept feeling called to use my voice for this new advocacy role I was handed and continue to grow the yoga studio where it can help others in a more impactful way. My love of writing and my comfort in public speaking also felt like it would go to waste if I didn't nurture that and use it for those who need someone to be a voice for them. It felt like staying solely in corporate would minimize that opportunity.

It wasn't just hard to walk away because of the financial impact. That was important, but I knew I would find a way to be scrappy the way I always had. It was harder to walk away without feeling like I was giving up. Was I saying that I couldn't balance it all? Was I throwing away an opportunity that a lot of women aren't given? I know it's not fair to put all of that pressure on myself, but the thoughts were there. But all I can do is put my efforts towards things I am truly passionate about and forge a path a different way. One that's more on my terms.

It took a long time to get here, but I am excited for this new venture. Trusting that it will all work out. Knowing that this was the better choice for my family. Just like when I received Rhea's diagnosis, the future seems so unknown yet so full of possibility.

Silver Linings:

- I am grateful to have had a career that helped provide for my family throughout the years, from the everyday to the big contributions.
- I am grateful to have been given the opportunity to hold a Vice President role, even if for just a couple of

years, because I am hopeful it paved the way for more in my company.

- I am grateful that I have a husband who supported me leaving my job and believing in the bigger things I could do.
- I am grateful to have the opportunity to put my family first and work around their schedule, especially having a child with extra needs.

Settling In

As I write this, my mom has been gone for just over a year. I wish I could say that getting through the first "firsts" without her feels like a relief, but the grief can shift in new ways. You can prepare yourself for birthdays and Christmas and other things being emotionally fraught the first time, but when they are over, and your grief is still there, it feels heavy. We have found really special ways to keep her memory alive, but the feeling of losing a mom is hard to move past. I'm not sure the grief ever goes away, and part of me doesn't want it to, because for grief to be gone, their memory might be as well. Grief carries with it the privilege of having loved someone so deeply.

Rhea is now two years old. There are things about her disability that get somewhat difficult as she becomes a toddler and I know that there are so many things ahead of us that will require hard work, patience and understanding. We have so much further to go and I still have an incredible amount to learn, but I am certain that this beautiful child has changed so much for me. I have found a new purpose in what I put my time and energy towards and how I parent my other girls. I'm learning to sit comfortably in Rhea's timeline, something at which an impatient person like myself was never good. Some milestones take a long time to get to, and I might feel somewhat impatient working on the same thing over and over, but I do not feel stress from the waiting. I know that she has things that she is really great at and others that don't come as easily and that's okay. Because of this, I find I'm listening more closely to the strengths and weaknesses of my other girls, and try to tune into their individual needs. It's a lens of motherhood I wish I had a long time ago.

My dreams for Rhea do not involve traditional things—not because they can't. As my imagination remains boundless, I don't believe for one second that she can't achieve anything she sets her mind to. Do I want Rhea to go to college? Of course I would be overjoyed for her, but I want that for Rhea if *she* wants it. She will have to work harder for things, so I want to make sure they are her objectives and not mine. My dream would be that she can live her purpose, be happy and fulfilled, whatever form that takes. My role is to support her and you can be sure I will be doing that.

The funny thing though? Most days I don't think much about Down syndrome when it comes to Rhea. Down syndrome is a huge part of our life because of the people we have met and the things we've devoted our time to, but I don't think of Down syndrome every time I look at Rhea or in the everyday moments. Life with her has become so "ordinary" that I forget that there are kids who don't have four therapies a week. I forget when milestones are typically met because I have gotten so used to Rhea's pace. I've gotten so immersed in the Down syndrome community that I am almost surprised when someone *doesn't* have a baby with an extra chromosome.

"Do you think people can see it?" I asked Raff one day.

"See what?" he replied.

"Down syndrome. Do you think total strangers know she has Down syndrome?"

It sounds like such a funny question - maybe with an obvious answer depending on who is responding

- but Down syndrome has become so typical to us that I forget in the everyday moments.

Such a change from where I thought things would be in October 2019.

Of course, I wouldn't be human if I didn't still worry about people discriminating against her. This Fall, we were at a local toy store. Rhea was yelling happily as she saw things that she wanted to touch. Not loud, but obvious. An older couple looked over at her and then quickly looked away. I knew they knew something was different. The noises she was making were only apparent to me when someone else started staring.

I wonder when she gets older, will she be treated differently because she isn't an adorable baby anymore. Will it still be cute if she's acting differently at a restaurant? Was the happy yelling she was doing at the toy store obnoxious or adorable? Will the people who say how amazing she is still think that way if we want her in their child's Kindergarten classroom? Would the people who "like" my content on social media consider her worthy of a job at their company someday?

I don't know the answers to these questions. I hope that with each bit of advocating and each advancement our society makes, that we will truly become a more inclusive world. It is my mission behind volunteering my time with organizations like the Down

Syndrome Diagnosis Network and co-founding Extra Lucky Moms with my friend Jess; a community platform for moms of all different disabilities. I'd love to get to a point where we are not told "I'm sorry" when receiving a disability diagnosis and just given support and encouragement. I'd love for a mom to feel fully celebrated and lifted up when she's in the thick of parenting a child with a disability…but also be able to vent about the hard parts without judgment.

I've been so humbled by my journey as an advocate for the Down syndrome community. Some days it's about education and speaking up, and other days it's about listening and learning. I know I haven't always and won't always get everything right, but I am committed to always growing in the process.

I know, as well, that no matter how beautiful things are, there will be hard days ahead of us. Days where we will struggle. Days where medical needs will be higher. Days where we have to fight for inclusion. Days where we have to push past the word "no." Days where we have to accept different paths and forgive adversity. Days where people are unkind. And days where we may have to turn the other cheek where transigent intolerance exists. But I know that we will get through it, and that's the difference from what I felt in those early days. Those struggles seemed like things that would break us, but the more I trust this journey, the more I learn from Rhea and the more in love with her I fall, I know we will be okay.

I have two Mantra bands that I never take off, both are lyrics from my favorite artists, and they read:

> **"Show a little faith, there's magic in the night."**
> **(Thunder Road, Bruce Springsteen)**
> **"All you need is love"**
> **(All You Need Is Love, The Beatles)**

Both quotes remind me that sometimes the most beautiful things come from hard times and that love is the underlying glue of life. My love for Sofia, Layla, Genevieve and Rhea was never dependent on how many chromosomes they had or what struggles might pop up in life. This journey of parenthood, and life in general, was never guaranteed to be a simple one. It's in those extraordinary moments where we learn, grow and love the most.

I've learned most of all that this one life we get to live is much more beautiful when we take the road less traveled, when we lean into the unknowns and when we always look for the silver linings.

Epilogue

I think back to the person I was when I was 33. Before the debilitating depression. Before my mom's health struggles. Before losing my mother-in-law. Before Down syndrome. Before Rhea's heart surgery. Before losing my mom.

I am not sure I would recognize that person anymore. She had not been through these upheavals; but she was in some ways so weak and so vulnerable.

While I would give anything to have the women I lost be here, each of the many experiences of the past six years shaped who I am today. Those experiences were encircled with lessons, growth and yes, silver linings. I am stronger. I am more confident. I have a louder voice. I know what's important. I am a better mother. I am full of gratitude in my bones, the way I always wanted.

I am in no way perfect. I do not have it all figured out. I do not have it all together. My car is a mess, my laundry piles up and I forget homework assignments and due dates and am horrible about replying to texts and emails. I won't always say the right thing and I will make mistakes.

But I will forever be grateful for every moment of this life.

We can't always control the journey, but if we can steer the ship, we can enjoy the ride.

Acknowledgements

To Tracey & Mary, your knowledge has been inval-
uable and I am grateful you have rooted for me
and helped me believe this book was possible.

To Jess, Lora, Sarah, Courtney, Megan, Cheryl and
Joanna. Thank you for being some of my favorite silver
linings on this journey. I am so grateful that our kids
brought us our friendships. I have loved laughing with
and leaning on you all.

To all of the children of the 2020 Lucky Mamas,
the heart mama group and the NJ Down syndrome
families. You motivate me daily and I can't wait to
watch you grow up. I will always believe that you *can*.

To the heart mamas who I have had the privilege
of sharing a journey with. Thank you for allowing me

to love and pray for your babies. You are all the fiercest mamas I have ever known.

To Kat, Karen, Sandi, Francesca, Francesca and Judy for being among the first people to show me that this journey would be ok. You set the tone with such simple words.

To Rhea's therapists: Alexis, Kayla, Nicole, Lori, Nicole, Nicole, Susan and Sue. Aside from my gratitude for loving and nurturing Rhea, you were an integral part of my journey these first couple of years parenting a child with a disability. You will all always be a part of our story.

To Rhea's cardiologist and the cardiology team at Columbia University Medical Center. Thank you could probably never be enough, but thank you for giving my daughter a chance at a beautiful life.

To Kristin and Carley, whose imprints are quite literally all over this book and behind the scenes. Thank you for always being my cheerleaders and making my dreams look prettier.

To Maura and Mike, your friendship will always be my most reliable source of laughter and support. You have been there with steadfast love through virtually every moment in this book. Thank you for growing with me and loving my kids as your own.

To my lifelong family and friends, from Bloomfield to Marist to Caldwell and beyond. I am fortunate that there are too many of you to name. Thank you for friendship through all seasons of life.

To Lauren, who always encourages my voice. You are an incredible sister and an even greater friend. You have taught me so much through your experiences, much like Mommy did. Thank you for the love you give to all of us.

To Mom, who I wish could have seen this day. Your presence is throughout this book much as it has been in so many big ways since you left. I know you would have enjoyed this moment so much and I can almost hear your voice saying so. I hope we are doing you proud. "In my life, I love you more."

To Dad, who will always be my first best friend. It is because of you that I found a love of writing and it's because of you that I had the audacity to think my writings could be a book for others to read. You were the first person who taught me that dreams don't have limits. You will always be my greatest teacher and within that you gave me the itch to always keep learning. Thank you for the time and energy you put into this book, and thank you for the countless ways you show up in my life.

To Raff, who believes in me most in this world. Thank you for always supporting my dreams from the beginning of our journey together. You are a great partner, friend and father and I am so grateful that you have been an unwavering pillar during all of these moments in this book. You held patience for me when I needed it most and waited for me to find myself in the way you knew I could.

To Sofia, Layla, Genevieve and Rhea. I am grateful beyond measure that I get to be your mom. Thank you for being my motivation, my book cover designers and for all the beautiful ways you've changed me. This is for you - you are the reason behind everything I do. I could do many things, but you will always be what I am most proud of. I hope you follow your dreams in whichever way life takes you. Be kind, be confident, be you.

About the Cover

This book is deeply personal for me, so it felt important for the cover to be representative of that. The
colors blue and yellow represent Down syndrome for
my daughter Rhea and the purple represents yoga, calm
and balance in my life.

The elements of the cover were shaded by my oldest three daughters Sofia, Layla and Genevieve and
digitally formatted into one picture by the incredibly
talented Kristin Broek. It was Kristin's idea to incorpo-
rate the girls' drawings into the cover and now I can't
imagine it any other way. They have created the color
in my life every day since they each arrived, and I love
that their work is the first thing you will see when you
look at this book.

About The Author

Taryn Lagonigro spent almost twenty years in the financial technology field with roles in project management, customer service, customer success and was most recently Vice President at a global organization. Taryn decided to step away in Fall of 2021 to focus on family, writing and entrepreneurship, but continues to remain a business strategy consultant.. Taryn is the mom to four daughters, the youngest of whom threw her into a world of advocacy when she was born with Down syndrome in March 2020. Taryn is the co-owner of Iris Yoga, a yoga studio in Bloomfield, New Jersey, and Extra Lucky Moms, an advocacy brand in the disability community. Taryn is certified in yoga and meditation and also volunteers for several Down syndrome organizations and nonprofits. Taryn's writings have been featured in several national publications and she has frequently been a guest on podcasts and television shows for topics relating to yoga, Down syndrome and parenting a child with a disability.

Taryn runs on coffee, wine and gratitude as she and her husband Raffaele are busy raising their four young daughters, Sofia, Layla, Genevieve and Rhea.

Made in the USA
Columbia, SC
20 September 2022

67671894R00100